SPALDING®

Winning Hockey

Bob Cielo

MASTERS PRESS

NTC/Contemporary Publishing Group

Library of Congress Cataloging-in-Publication Data

Cielo, Bob.
    Winning Hockey / Bob Cielo.
       p.   cm. — (Spalding sports library)
    At head of title: Spalding
    ISBN 1-57028-076-2
    1. Hockey.   2. Hockey—Coaching.   I. Title.   II. Series.
GV847.C55   1996
796.962—dc20   96-2011
                                           CIP

A Masters Press book
Published by Contemporary Books
A division of NTC/Contemporary Publishing Group, Inc.
4255 West Touhy Avenue, Lincolnwood (Chicago), Illinois 60646-1975 U.S.A.
Printed in the United States of America
International Standard Book Number: 1-57028-076-2

20   19   18   17   16   15   14   13   12   11   10   9   8   7   6   5   4   3

Table of Contents

Foreword

The game of hockey today is a much different game than that of many years ago. Rules have changed, rinks may be larger, and players are bigger and stronger, to name just a few of the changes that we have seen in recent years. But the job of the coach still includes two very important functions. The coach must teach the fundamentals of the game. Skating, puck handling, shooting, passing, and checking must be taught well so a player has a chance for progress and to enjoy the game. A coach must also instruct his players on the system of play that they will utilize throughout the season or on a given night. A player still asks the same questions as he did a long time ago: "Where am I going?", "What do I do when I get there?", "Why am I doing this?". In short, a player needs to know the system or style his team will use and what his role or job description is in that system.

No matter what the team sport may be, a carefully devised method must be used so that all the players know what is expected of them as the team moves up and down the ice or playing field.

I believe that players want to know what to do and where to go, and it is the coach who must teach and reinforce this. You see young baseball players react and move into position when a ball is hit.... You see young football players following a play book.... How about our young hockey players?

Bob Cielo's book addresses our game — and how to play it as a team. It includes simple terms with very good diagrams to explain each and every system. It can serve any coach who wants to know about hockey played in each and every zone. A coach can use this resource throughout the season to adjust, change, or re-examine his systems. It is a good layman's book — one that will allow the coach to answer a lot of the what, where, and why questions.

— *Jon Christiano,*
Coaching Staff, Florida Panthers

Credits:

Front cover design by Christy Pierce

Cover photos © Frank Howard

Edited by Kathleen Prata

Proofread by Pat Brady

Diagrams by Scott Stadler and Phil Velikan

Introduction

T his book is not an attempt to provide revolutionary material intended to "replace" already existing philosophy, or tactical design, towards the game of ice hockey. Instead, a more humble approach has been taken. It is realized that the art of successfully coaching involves a comprehensive assortment of reading, observing, teaching, and both game and practice experience. More often than not, there are no shortcuts. Even the most experienced of coaches can learn something new with each game played, each new practice designed, and each piece of literature added to their library. This book is dedicated to those who recognize this, and continue to nourish their creative and intellectual appetites, while attempting to learn more about a sport which we so openly love.

Although designed as a review, this book includes many new systems and strategies which will "enhance" the already pre-established tactics of many coaches. It is not intended to revolutionize, but simply to contribute and assist. If only one new piece of information is gained and successfully transferred to the ice, this book has fulfilled its purpose. In addition, the material is presented in a manner inviting all coaches to modify or adapt to their needs and talents. The book's layout is designed to simulate the flow of play in an actual game.

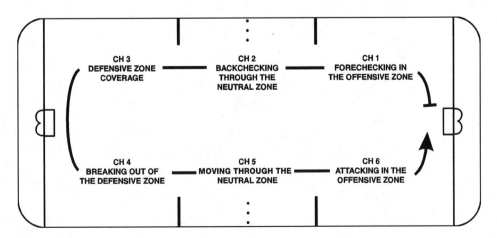

Note how this tactic allows for a) system coverage, and b) transfer from book to ice in a more organized fashion. Coaches will find this format much easier to teach, versus jumping from zone to zone. Rather than dictating player movement, coaches are called upon to become more creative in their inputs. In the overall picture, this only adds to the game itself. I ask all who read this book not to approach it as a "cure-all," but as a contribution to the comprehensive process which forever makes us "students" of the game.

KEY:

OZ - OFFENSIVE ZONE
NZ - NEUTRAL ZONE
DZ - DEFENSIVE ZONE

F1 - LEFT WING
F2 - CENTER
F3 - RIGHT WING
D1 - LEFT DEFENSEMAN
D2 - RIGHT DEFENSEMAN
G - GOALTENDER

XF - OPPOSING FORWARD
XD - OPPOSING DEFENSEMAN

\- SKATING FORWARDS

\- SKATING BACKWARDS

\- SKATING WITH PUCK CONTROL

\- A PASS

\- A SHOT

\- AN ABRUPT STOP

Dedication

"The U.S. is depending a little too much on Jim Craig; he's making too many big ... ERUZIONE!!!" — Ken Dryden and Al Michaels, 1980

A memory that will live forever

SECTION 1
Defensive Team Play

During his playing career, Bill Nyrop won three Stanley Cups with the Montreal Candiens. I was fortunate to skate for him and experience all the knowledge and expertise he had to offer. He once told us, "Offense can be recruited, but defense must be taught and learned." In retrospect, there is indeed validity to this statement. Defensive team play in today's version of ice hockey is similar to what it always has been — namely, play the man while receiving the support needed to gain puck control. As expected, both team positioning and individual effort are significant factors in whether puck control is gained or relenquished.

The "team play" aspect is the motivation behind writing this book. It represents why we as coaches take notes on every game we see. The defensive system implemented requires teaching clear and specific principles. However, the system is worthless if not executed properly. It is the aspect of "individual effort" from which proper execution is fueled.

Although teaching team play includes a tremendous amount of the coaching staff's duties, it is only half the battle. The work ethic component within each players' personality also needs to be developed. Coaches can continuously lecture and diagram external strategic movements. However, the internal drive that motivates players to execute the plays is modeled after the dedication and commitment of the coach. This is no more evident than in establishing a disciplined defensive system. After all, we cannot move offensively until we have gained control of the puck.

1

Forechecking in the Offensive Zone

"The use of force alone is but temporary. It may subdue for a moment; but it does not remove the necessity of subduing again."
— H. Goldsmith, The Vicar of Wakefield

Somewhere along the line, young players have absorbed the notion of reacting "after" the pass is completed, rather than reading, forcing, and anticipating the play. Simply put, it is the combination of proper positioning and anticipation which enables us to execute our movements faster than the opposition. Thus, the speed accompanied by knowing where to go, awards us a greatly enhanced opportunity to nullify movements made by our opponents. For example, our forwards (F) have been taught to immediately recognize the three prominent passing options available to the opposition's defenseman (Xd), having gained possession of the puck deep in his own zone. (See Figures 1.1, 1.2, and 1.3.)

1. Reversing the play: a) Pass to partner   b) Wrap to far wing
2. Strong-side outlet
3. Middle lane outlet

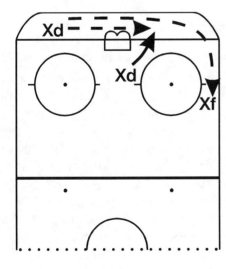

Figure 1.1

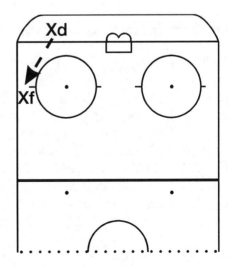

Figure 1.2

Winning Hockey

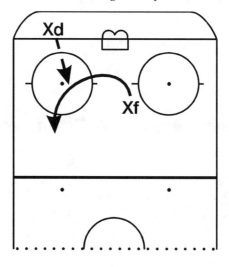

Figure 1.3

The proper positioning of our forwards in the offensive zone (OZ), permits a quick transition which can easily prevent the success of each above-diagrammed option. This proper positioning involves the tactical strategies of various forechecking systems. As we begin to examine this very important aspect of the game, let us assume that Xd continues to maintain puck control in the OZ. Depending on the present situation (score, players on the ice, time left in the period, etc.), different forechecking schemes can be employed. The three basic systems detailed in this section differ in their level of "aggressiveness." If the primary goal of regaining puck control is not jeopardized, adaptation and/or modification regarding the specific movements of individual players within the system is encouraged.

Logo Principle: "Patience vs. Pressure"

Is the logo on Xd's jersey visible to our first forechecker as he enters the OZ?

In attempts to frustrate opponents, it is not uncommon for coaches to assign different forechecking schemes to different lines. While still playing, I remember one of our lines being especially physical. If the opportunity presented itself, this particular line was given the green light to aggressively forecheck two men deep, regardless of the situation. By finishing their checks in the OZ, they began to wear down Xd and intimidate them into forcing the puck. This "opportunity" stems from a guideline that has been followed from the days of "Eddie Shore and old-time hockey." Namely, if the logo on the opposition's jersey is not visible to our forwards as they enter the OZ, Xd have not had time to establish puck control. Thus, their breakout has not yet been set up, and our forecheckers can pressure aggressively. Conversely, if the logo on the opposition's jersey is visible to our forwards as they enter the OZ, Xd is most likely facing up ice with control of the puck. The forwards should react accordingly, by attempting to position themselves between the puck and their assignments dictated by that particular forechecking scheme.

This guideline can be used to assist in determining which approach to exercise, while installing both uniformity and consistency to player movement in the OZ.

Now that we have acknowledged that different scenarios warrant different forechecking systems, let us begin to examine the systems themselves. Before commencing, it is important to re-emphasize the movement of our first forechecker (F2) as he converges on the opposition. Instruct forwards neither to approach the puck carrier head on, nor station themselves in line with the center of the net. Instead, approach from a slight angle and/or set up off one post, forcing puck movement to one side of the ice. This is referred to as "flushing" the opposition and reduces the need for teammates to guess where the puck is going. We can better anticipate our players' reactions and movement is much quicker.

Game Scenario:

After dumping the puck deep, the logo on Xd's jersey *is* visible to our first forechecker as he enters the OZ.

Because the logo is visible, Xd is facing up ice and most likely has had the opportunity to analyze his options. Rather than apply immediate pressure and risk getting caught in deep, we can employ one of the following set forechecks. Here, our goal is to force a turnover by manipulating the opposition's breakout into an area already occupied by our teammates.

1-2-2 Wide

The distinguishing characteristic of this 1-man forecheck, is the positional assumption of the three forwards (F1, F2, & F3). Because it is designated as a "wide" alignment, the primary objective is to shut down those passing lanes to the outside. Thus, the opposition will be forced to use passing options through their own slot area. Should a pass be mishandled or thrown beyond the reach of the intended target, a turnover in this area runs the risk of surrendering an immediate scoring opportunity. It is diagrammed in Figure 1.4.

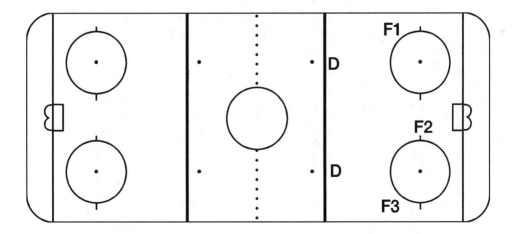

Figure 1.4

It is the positioning of F1 and F3 which affix the term "wide" to this forecheck. Note how they set up within the outside lanes. The responsibility of these two forwards is to clog breakout options designed along the boards. By shutting down these outside lanes, passes are forced through the middle. Even if the opposing puck-side forwards interchange, F1 and F3 should maintain these lanes. Remember, our goal here is to force puck movement through the slot area.

F2 attempts to flush the puck carrier to one side. Most likely, the opposing center will curl in support of the puck carrier's movement. While this is occurring, both of our defensemen have established control of the inside lanes along the blueline. Because our defensemen (D) are aware of the limited passing lanes (up the middle), the one positioned on the side to which the puck-receiving Xf is curling can step up in anticipation of the pass. (See Figure 1.5.)

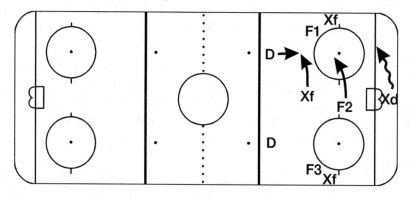

Figure 1.5

1-2-2 Tight

As can be expected, this forechecking approach differs from the "1-2-2 Wide", in its positioning of both forwards and defensemen. Thus, the objective is different. Rather than clogging up the outside lanes, F1 and F3 position themselves within the inside lanes. Conversely, both D set up along the blue line a bit wider than usual. Because our forwards are covering the middle lanes and any opposing forward (Xf) curling through this area, most breakouts will be directed to players situated along the boards. (See Figure 1.6.)

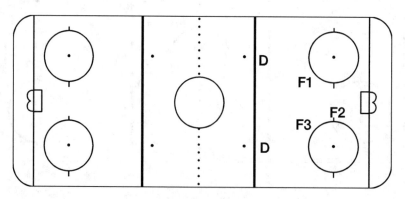

Figure 1.6

As before, F2 fulfills his role of flushing the puck carrier to commit to one side. With no options available through the middle, Xd is forced to use the outside lanes. Because our D are aware of these limited passing options (to the outside), their positioning allows for an aggressive pinch. Once again, we have successfully manipulated the flow of play to one side of the ice, making it easier for our forecheckers to anticipate and react. (See Figure 1.7.) If possible, have our D play their "on-side" at the points. It is much easier to keep pucks in the zone when using one's forehand.

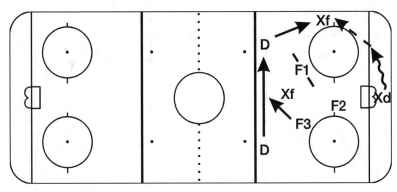

Figure 1.7

1-3-1 Post

This forechecking approach is incorporated within many European systems. Note how the weak side D has to post up in the OZ. It is believed to be based, in part, on years of success in the sport of soccer. (See Figure 1.8.)

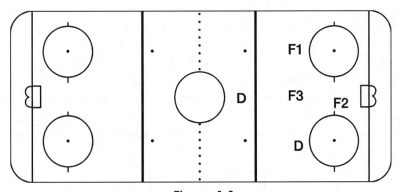

Figure 1.8

Like the previous 1-man forechecks described, F2 does not immediately pressure the puck carrier. Again, he positions himself off one post in front of the opposition's net. It is hypothesized that Xd will view this half-step as an open passing lane along the boards. However, F2's teammates recognize that his original positioning has helped manipulate the direction of the opposition's breakout and they react accordingly. This forecheck calls for three other players positioned in the OZ to support the movement of the first, each with specific responsibilities. Ideally, with one D vacating the point and assuming a position inside the blue line, we would like F2 to set up off that same side post. Thus, we flush the puck towards an area occupied by our forwards. The subsequent movement following the first pass enables the far side D to resume his position along the blue line.

For example, F2 has succeeded in flushing the breakout to one side, while his positioning in front subsequently blocks the far passing lane. F1 is responsible for the outside lanes and is in position to quickly pinch on the puck receiving Xf. F3 shuts down the middle by picking up any Xf curling through that area as an outlet or option. Once the puck is on its way to the boards, both D can assume their proper positioning on the blue line. (See Figure 1.9.)

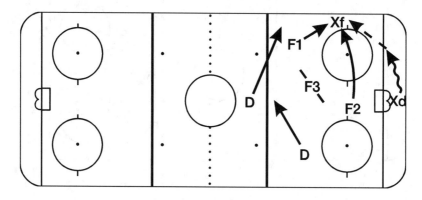

Figure 1.9

Neutral Zone Trap

Although used by the great Montreal Canadian teams of the 1970's, recent successful application by the New Jersey Devils and Florida Panthers has promoted the neutral zone (NZ) trap back into prominence. Considered conservative in preliminary design, its objective is the same as all other forechecks. However, the turnovers which may result do not occur deep in the OZ. Instead, if executed properly, this approach has proven quite successful in creating turnovers inside the neutral zone. Because it is difficult to break out against and does not trap any forwards in deep, this forecheck is being increasingly employed in situations involving the protection of a lead and/or following a dump and change. In both scenarios, we force the opposition's breakout to come through us. The positioning of all five players in front of the puck poses little or no threat of surrendering an odd-man rush. (See Figure 1.10.)

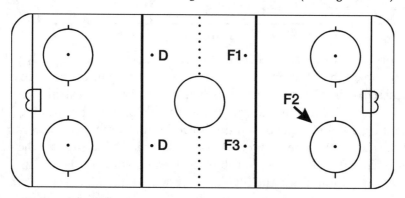

Figure 1.10

F2 positions himself off one post approximately halfway in to the OZ. F1 and F3 set up just outside the opposition's blue line. Similarly, both D set up just outside the red line.

Whether Xd carries or passes the puck is irrelevant. Once the outside lane commitment has been made, F2 applies pressure by converging from an inside angle. As the puck carrier approaches the blue line, he will also be confronted by the puck side wing (here, F1) stepping up. Both F1 and F3 position their sticks so that the blades occupy the seam between them. This helps force puck movement to the outside. F3 assumes the responsibility for middle lane coverage. The opposite side D remains in position to cover the far lane. If executed properly, the puck carrier will be forced to play the puck back into his own zone or attempt a low percentage cross-ice pass through several of our players. Regardless, the man-advantage situation presented by F2 and F1 converging on the puck carrier should negate any opportunity to headman the puck. (See Figure 1.11.)

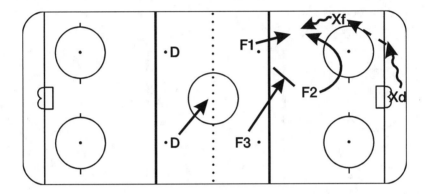

Figure 1.11

If we are successful in causing a NZ turnover and gain control of the puck, look to regroup with F3 relocating in the far lane. Once away from the traffic jam created by this setup, coaches can design movements to complement this quick transition from defense to offense (refer to Chapter 5). (See Figure 1.12.)

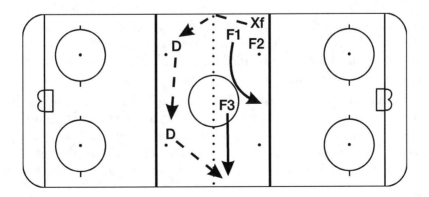

Figure 1.12

Game Scenario:

After dumping the puck deep, the logo on Xd's jersey *is not* visible to our first forechecker as he enters the OZ.

Because the logo is not visible, Xd is not facing up ice and has not yet had the opportunity to analyze his options. Rather than give the opposition time to set up their breakout, applying immediate pressure creates turnovers by forcing puck movement.

1-Man Flush

This forechecking approach is very common among prep school and college coaches. It too is consistent with the theme of flushing the puck carrier to commit one way. The objective is to anticipate and numerically overload one side of the ice. Due to the movements of F2, both F1 and F3 may need to shift lanes. The preliminary alignment is shown in Figure 1.13.

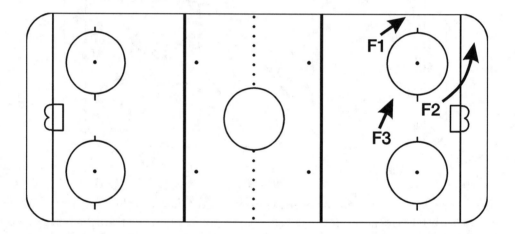

Figure 1.13

F2 flushes the puck carrier to one side. By approaching from an inside angle, we establish our positioning in the middle lane and force puck movement up the boards. Note that his path takes him into the corner, where if needed, he can assume an offensive role. F1 immediately heads to the primary outlet area along the near boards, where Xw is positioned (most likely, around the hash marks). F3, in turn, heads for the slot in an attempt to take away the middle lane options.

The key to success with this forecheck is the timing of F1 to the boards. If too early, the present puck carrier may decide to continue carrying the puck. It is important that players do not converge to the outside until the commitment has been made (i.e. once the puck leaves the stick of Xd). Even if the pass is completed along the outside lane, F1 can provide immediate pressure with no headman outlets available. (See Figure 1.14.)

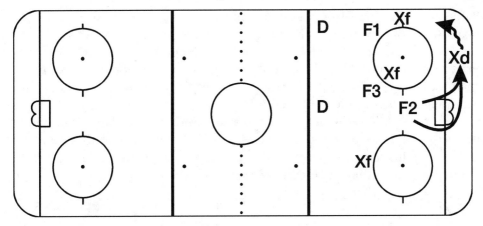

Figure 1.14

Should we cause a turnover along these boards, remember that we have F2 waiting in the corner to assume an offensive role. If we can slide the puck to him, a play can be designed with F1 and F3 converging on the net.

2-Man Flush

This forecheck is simply a more aggressive version of the "1-Man Flush." As its title indicates, the play is designed to have two forwards put pressure on the puck carrier. Whereas the 1-man flush assigns F1 to the near boards, here he is directed to challenge the oncoming puck carrier being flushed by F2. F3 can be assigned to pressure the pass recipient along the boards or maintain responsibility for the high slot (middle lanes). Should the latter be instructed, the D on that side must compensate for the coverage sacrificed along the outside lanes by sending F1 in deep. This is accomplished by aggressively pinching down low. As his partner shifts to cover the vacated point, F3 slides back from the high slot to the blue line. (See Figure 1.15.)

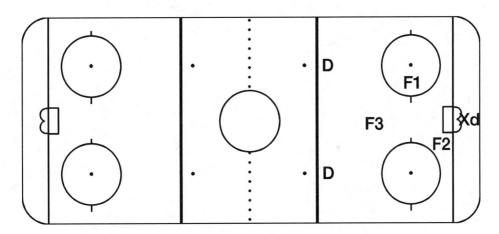

Figure 1.15

Remember, sending F1 down deep is most productive when the opposition has not had the opportunity to set up (i.e. puck control is not yet established, Xd is not facing up ice, Xf are still returning from the neutral zone, etc.). Because the forecheckers both pursue and confront the puck carrier, the objective is to force the play "through" one of them. For example, F2 approaches the puck carrier from an outside angle, forcing the play behind the net into an oncoming F1. The puck carrier must decide whether to attempt to skate around F1 or slide a pass by him. In most cases, the second of these options will be taken. It is at this point that F3 crashes, or if instructed otherwise, the puck-side D pinch while his teammates rotate in support of this movement. (See Figure 1.16.)

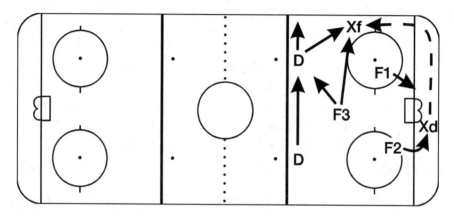

Figure 1.16

Should the puck be turned over either down low or along the boards, coaches must keep in mind the positioning of the forwards. Because at least two will have penetrated deep, coaches may want to design offensive counterattacks from that area. It makes little sense, unless wide open, to risk trapping two to three men in deep by forcing a pass back to our points (especially since one of them may not be a defenseman, but F3 covering back).

Forechecking in the Offensive Zone: A Summary

1. Although in the OZ, forechecking entails a quick transition from offensive to defensive play. Learn to react before the pass ... rather than after it.
2. Our goal: To create a turnover and gain puck control.
3. F2: If possible, do not confront the puck carrier head on. Approaching from an angle makes it much easier for the support forwards (F1 & F3) to anticipate the direction in which the play will be flushed.

Logo Principle:

Is the logo on Xd's jersey visible to our first forechecker?

- Being able to see the logo connotes that Xd is facing up ice and has been able to analyze his options .... Thus, a forecheck designed to manipulate puck movement should be set up.
- Not being able to see the logo signals that Xd is not facing up ice and has not been able to evaluate his options. Thus, a forecheck designed to pressure the puck carrier and force puck movement should be employed.

If the logo is visible ... Patience

- 1-2-2 Wide: Wide positioning of F1 & F3 forces breakout through slot (middle lanes).
- 1-2-2 Tight: Tight positioning of F1 & F3 forces breakout up boards (outside lanes).
- 1-3-1 Post: Positioning of one deep forward and three players inside blue line confronts breakout at the extended zone.
- NZ Trap: Positioning of support unit in NZ traps puck to one side, with no opportunity to headman.

If the logo is not visible ... Pressure

- 1-Man Flush: Areas overloaded force puck movement into lanes occupied by support forwards.
- 2-Man Flush: Areas overloaded force puck movement into second forechecker.

The Key to Pinching

Only if supported by a forward in the high slot can our D pinch. If the puck gets by him, tie Xf up along the boards and allow teammates to retrieve puck.

- Regardless of the forecheck employed, at least one F must be in position to penetrate down low in anticipation of a turnover. Thus if we gain control of the puck, we have the option of firing it in deep with an immediate presence.

Remember: Attempt to establish your forechecking game IMMEDIATELY.

2

Backchecking through the Neutral Zone

"In doing what we ought, we deserve no praise ... because it is our duty." — St. Augustine, Confessions, BK. X

Lane Responsibilities

For the purpose of initiating a discussion on defensive coverage, let us assume that puck control has been established by the opposition following a successful breakout from their own zone. As the puck approaches the "extended" NZ, most proficient defensive strategies are derived from the assignments created by specific "lane" responsibilities. (See Figure 2.1.)

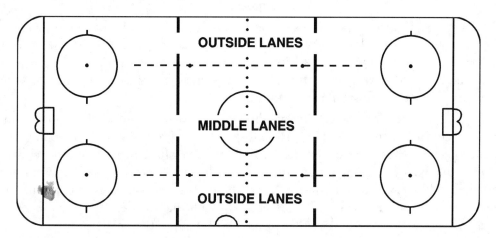

Figure 2.1

Note that the responsibilities of both defensemen include the puck carrier and those forwards (Xf) which curl to the middle in support of his movements. This comprises the middle lanes throughout the entire neutral zone. Here, our defensemen play on their respective sides of the ice and should not cross into their partners' territory. This is most successfully accomplished by the fine art of "communication."

As with all defensive team play, teach players to "verbally" mark their assignments by yelling out the number or position before locking on. Using terms such as "puck

17

carrier," "wide man," and/or "trailer," helps to install both confidence and uniformity to the movement of the entire unit.

By design, the first two backchecking forwards (F1 and F3) into the neutral zone attempt to shut down the outside passing lanes. Teach players to approach the opposition from an angle. Here, an inside angle flushes Xf wide and outside. This line establishes positioning between the puck carrier and his passing options. Should the opposing forwards interchange, maintain control of the outside lanes. This forces penetration through the defense. If a man-advantage situation is created, our weak side forward can extend his lane coverage from one-third to one-half of the ice. (See Figure 2.2.)

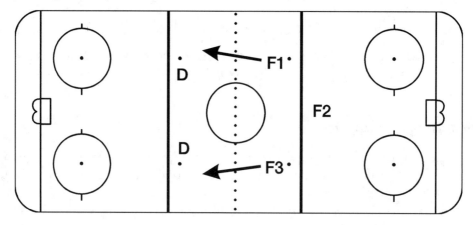

Figure 2.2

Remember, it is the opposition's support forwards (Xf) who will attempt to accelerate through the neutral zone. When backchecking, always attempt to remain to the inside of, and no further than a stick length, from your assignment. If you can get to our blue line before Xf, pivot and face him. It is much easier to see and hold up your assignment versus having your back to him.

Regardless of the forecheck used, we should have at least one F in the high slot until we gain control of the puck. His positioning enables him to support a pinching D, as well as pick up the wide man or trailer. If an unsuccessful 2-man forecheck results in two of our forwards being caught in deep, the high forward (F3) should attempt to neutralize the rush. If behind the puck and chasing a man-advantage situation (3 on 2, etc.), the first forward back can come back through the middle. As we will later see, most offensive attacks involving three men will assume the shape of a triangle. By backchecking through the middle lane, we will pressure the often dangerous high man or trailer. Thus our D can concentrate on the puck carrier and those players driving to the net. If at puck level and facing an even-man situation, the first forward back will "lock on" to the wide option. Again, allowing our D to concentrate on the puck carrier. (See Figure 2.3.)

Closing at least one lane considerably reduces the opposition's working area, limits their support options, and subsequently enables our defense to play more aggressively. Similarly, our second forward back into the play (F1) is responsible for the opposite side wing.

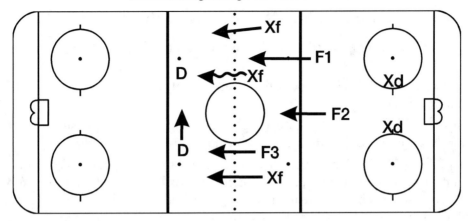

Figure 2.3

In each scenario, the responsibility of our last forward back (F2) through the neutral zone is threefold:

1. By skating up the middle, his positioning between the puck carrier and the defensemen (Xd) prevents the opportunity for "regrouping" by the opposition. The area established and maintained by this forward includes that between one's own net and Xd.

2. If one of their defensemen jumps into the rush or attempts to assume an offensive role, the area occupied by this same forward should negate a man-advantage situation due to the ease in which the opposing defenseman can be picked up (or covered).

3. Should a turnover occur, this same forward is now in position to assume the third of his responsibilities — namely, to exist as a rapid offensive transition outlet. Because ice hockey is a game that often involves "thinking ahead," it is strategically sound to have at least one forward always "in position" to quickly assume an offensive role. Take, for example, Pittsburgh Penguin Mario Lemieux, renowned as one of the most dangerous offensive players in the world, who continually finds ways to get open. When watching a game, it is obvious when Mario's line is on the ice and obvious to most coaching staffs when his line is due up. Undoubtedly, a tremendous amount of thinking is put into shutting him down. Yet, we continually see him on the highlight reels receiving breakaway pass after breakaway pass. How is one of the biggest and most respected players in the NHL allowed to continually sneak behind one's defense? Because Mario Lemieux is able to "think ahead" as well as anyone ever to play the game.

Backchecking through the Neutral Zone: A Summary

Both Defensemen: Responsible for the puck carrier and immediate support forwards (Inside lanes)

First two Forwards back: Responsible for additional and/or secondary support (Outside lanes/trailer)

Last Forward back: 1) Prevent Regrouping 2) Responsible for opposing defenseman joining the rush 3) Assume an offensive role upon a turnover (Middle lane)

"Stepping up" isn't restricted to the puck carrier, but passing options as well. If you are supported, step up in anticipation of headman passes. Remember, headman passes may be coming from behind the intended target. In addition to being able to anticipate the play before you, Xf may have to take his eyes off you and turn his head to face the pass.

Prevent Forecheck:

When coming back through the NZ, "hold up" your assignments. Give teammates time to retrieve the puck, face up ice and analyze their options.

- Forwards hold up Xf, and give our Defense time.
- Defense hold up Xf, and give our Goaltender time.

3

Defensive Zone Coverage

"Tho'
We are not now that strength which
in old days
Moved Earth and Heaven: that which
we are we are;
One equal temper of heroic hearts,
Made weak by time and fate, but
strong in will
To strive, to seek, to find, and not to yield."
                    —Lord Alford Tennyson, Ulysses

Discipline is vital to success in the defensive zone, more than anywhere on the ice. With discipline comes execution, and with execution comes success. By discipline, I mean knowing your roles and responsibilities. Too often goals are preceded by what play-by-play commentators note as "teams running around in their own zone." Should the opposition establish puck control inside our blue line, each player must realize that he has specific responsibilities. These do not include overloading or flooding an area until "after" the opposition's rush is halted by our successfully tying up the puck-controlling forward. These more aggressive primary movements must be preceded by tactical secondary movements which include the proper positioning of players for support and backup.

Convergence

Many coaches shudder at the thought of this word when applied to defensive zone play. It is often misinterpreted as "caving in" or "collapsing." Literally and strategically, the word convergence denotes a "merge, unity, and/or coming together." Its tactical application in the DZ may not be as concentrated or aggressive as in the OZ, but there exist similarities in the roles and movement of players.

Game Scenario:

The opposition is approaching our zone with puck control.

Unless facing a man-advantage rush, we do not want to voluntarily surrender the blue line. With adequate support (i.e. an even man rush or with a backchecker present), the puck-side D should step up in an attempt to force the play. His partner (D2) becomes responsible for retrieving the puck. Because the lane coverage system implemented in the NZ is extended and applied within the DZ, D2 can immediately look to feed the outside lanes. In addition to providing transition outlets, the positioning of these first two forwards coming back through the outside lanes creates a funnel shape. The purpose of a funnel is to filter out or impede the access of "undesirable elements" should Xf maintain puck control. (See Figure 3.1.)

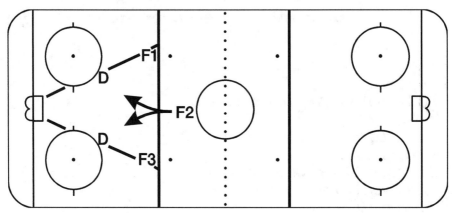

Figure 3.1

From a defensive posture, note how the positioning of the first two forwards coming back (F1 and F3) prohibit passing options to the outside by staying between their assignments and the puck carrier. With only the middle lanes open, the puck carrier is flushed into penetrating at a man-disadvantage situation (1 on 2). Because both the D and F's know their own roles, as well as what to expect from each other, there is less risk of a miscommunication resulting in two men chasing the puck carrier while leaving a wide man free. Due to the interchanging of position between the NZ and DZ, players may need to reaffirm their coverage by again "verbally marking" their assignments.

As the puck carrier crosses into the OZ, he will find himself trapped. Since our forwards have forced the play to the middle by remaining between their assignments and the puck, there exist no options. It is now detrimental to regroup for risk of surrendering the zone gained. If instructed, the third forward coming back (F2) can now offer defensive support down low. It is important that the last two forwards do not allow themselves to get sucked down below the top of the face-off circles. The weak-side wing (here, F3) can simply relinquish coverage of Xf to the D on that same side. However, should the last man back represent our center, note how a quick rotation may need to be executed with the puck-side wing (F1). (See Figure 3.2.) With the puck deep in the DZ, our center and puck-side D can pick up the puckcarrier and immediate support, while our opposite D picks up the weak-side option. Both wings can now slide out and assume responsibility for the opposition's points.

In the situation presented in Figure 3.2, the puck carrier must choose one of two options: a) attempt to penetrate the slot alone versus two defensemen; or, b) attempt to go outside because of the angular and oncoming pressure. Assigning responsibility of the support options to the forwards allows the defensemen to concentrate on this puck carrier. Even if passing or skating to an outside lane is accomplished, further puck penetration would be from an angle much easier for our goaltender to handle. Flushing

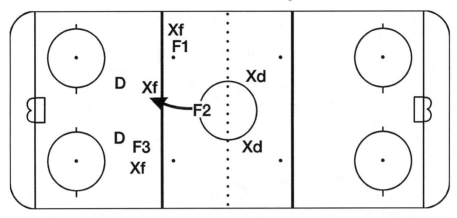

Figure 3.2

and/or angling the play to the perimeter like this also means that any additional passes attempted must now find their way back through the sticks and bodies of our players converging into, or already occupying, this area. From a defensive point of view, control of this middle area is vital. At some point, the opposition will attempt to move the puck from the perimeter ... inward. Proper positioning (versus "running around") is the key to thwarting such attempts. The assignments created by this system comply with those most fundamentally sound. Although there does exist some proximal areas of overlap, the general responsibilities in the DZ are shown in Figure 3.3.

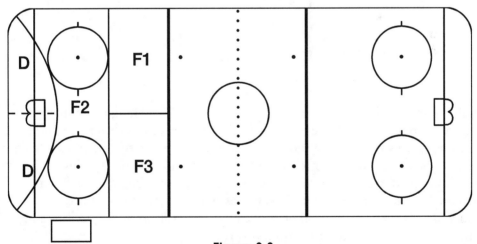

Figure 3.3

Both control and coverage of the slot area are a priority. Once again, the responsibilities are divided into zonal areas in accordance with the principle that "patience and positioning precede punishment." Proper positioning may take a second to set up, but is conducive and supportive for more aggressive play to commence. For example, because the D are aware of both their own and the Fs' responsibilities, they can play the puck carrier with the confidence of knowing that their teammates will respond "in support" of this initiating movement. This extinguishes tentative movements and hesitation caused by the fear that someone, somewhere has been left uncovered.

Although our ultimate goal is to force a turnover, we cannot gamble to the extent of conceding higher quality scoring opportunities to the opposition. Our goaltenders can bail us out of only so many predicaments. With proper positioning established, loose pucks following aggressive play have a greater chance of being retrieved by one of our supporting players. In such cases, we can expect overlap within the above zones. The most significant area involves the presence of F2 behind the goal line after the puck carrier has been tied up.

Box + 1

Our discussion of defensive positioning should the opposition cross into our zone is only partially complete to this point. The 45 degree triangle, or funnel, is designed to force the rush either into the defensemen or out to the perimeter. But what if puck control is established deep in one of the corners? What defensive formation should be assumed in this situation? (See Figure 3.4.)

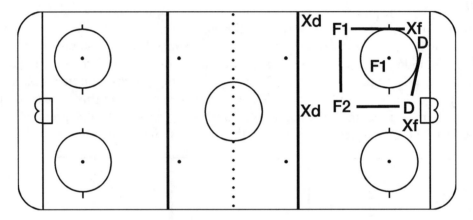

Figure 3.4

Ideally, our funnel is transformed into a box formation. Here, our wings cover the points, while our defensemen are responsible for the area immediately around the net. In most cases, this will include the puck carrier (here, along the side boards) and any support forward attempting to set up in front. Note that the positioning of X's third forward is limited to a) the slot area, b) behind the net, or c) supporting down low. F2, represented as the "+1," attempts to gain positioning between X's third forward and the puck by shadowing his assignment until the puck carrier is tied up. Note how the positioning of all five players continues to comply with the more general defensive zonal responsibilities illustrated in Figure 3.3.

Game Scenario:

The opposition has established puck control deep in our zone.

The strong-side D does not approach the puck carrier head on, but attempts to approach from an inside angle. By doing so, the puck carrier is flushed towards the boards and away from the net. Watch for "cycling" to develop between the deep puck carrier and any support forward which may be positioned at the top of the face-off circle on that side. To prevent this, or any type of accelerated movement from the corner (or outside perimeter), two things must occur. First, the strong-side D does not allow the puck carrier the freedom to pass and skate. Our defensemen need to tie their men up to take opposing players out of the play. Second, the deep forward back (F2) must gain position between the puck carrier and the nearest support option. If puck control has been established down low by the opposition, this player will undoubtedly attempt to set up in close proximity. F2 is responsible and must stay with him. Should our D be successful in tying up the puck carrier, it becomes the responsibility of our nearest forward (in most cases, F2) to retrieve the loose puck. In addition to the defensive advantages (i.e. blocking passes, clogging skating lanes, etc.), the transitional advantage gained by having F2 assume a position between the puck carrier and nearest support forward enables us to get to the puck first.

The weak-side D positions himself in front of the net and is responsible for any Xf attempting to set up in the slot. If the puck carrier is able to escape and attempts to reverse the play by skating behind the net, D1 must be well practiced in whether to maintain pursuit or relinquish coverage to D2 in front. Remember, only if in "immediate contact" should D1 stay with the puck carrier. Much playing confidence, especially around one's own goal, is rooted in the consistency of knowing what to do ... and when to do it.

However, the coordinated movements of our D need not be limited to defensive play. Look to include the weak-side D in the transition following a turnover. For example, if one of our forwards is successful in digging a loose puck out of the corner, the weak-side D can assume an offensive role by moving off the near post and/or slipping behind the net as a "reverse" tactic to slide play to open ice. Similarly, look for this same D to jump into the breakout should two Xf get caught deep in our zone. (See Figure 3.5.)

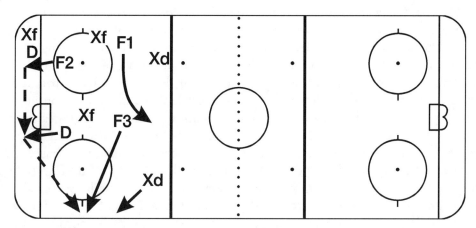

Figure 3.5

This is what makes players like Chris Chelios and Paul Coffey so invaluable. Although defensemen, they have developed the offensive skills needed to help their team on both sides of the puck.

Referring back to Figure 3.4, the two high forwards (F1 and F3) are responsible for covering the points. Thus, both players should never simultaneously allow themselves to get sucked in below the top of the face-off circles. With the exception of the weak-side wing dropping into the high slot to offer support to that area, there exist two scenarios for which these forwards are permitted to support in deep. The first defends against a potential scoring threat. Should either of the opposition's defensemen drive to the net looking for a pass from down low, coverage remains the responsibility of the high forward on that side of the ice ... even into the slot area. Failure to lock on to one's assignment creates a man-advantage situation for the opposition in front of our own net. (See Figure 3.6.)

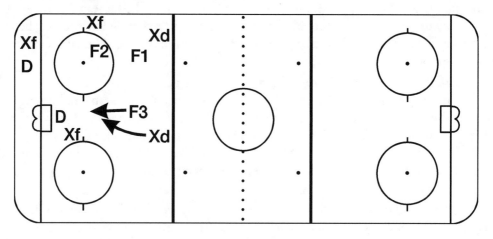

Figure 3.6

The second scenario centers around the capricious assumption that many turnovers in our favor will result from one D tying up the puck carrier, while the nearest forward (F2) will be in position to retrieve the puck first. Because life is not always so predictable, we would be wise in preparing for alternate outcomes. Whether unintentional or designed, there may be an attempt to reverse the play by throwing the puck around the net into the far corner. The effectiveness of this tactic, should an opposing player be the first to reach the puck, requires a rotation of our defensive alignment to the other side of the ice. Depending on the positioning of our deep forward, our rotation may include sending a far-side high forward to the corner. Once the opposition no longer has clear puck control in our zone, we need not limit movement to that area above the hash marks. For example, if F2 is battling along the left corner boards and the puck is thrown to the opposite corner, what is our best chance of getting there first? If a clear lane does not exist behind the net, it may prove quicker to send F3 in from the point area. If so, secondary support movements follow the rotation of a large triangle, with the weak-side forward sliding "over" to the area vacated by F3, and the previously deep forward sliding "out" to the area vacated by F1. Note that such coordinated movements provide both puck-side (immediate) and middle lane (secondary) support. (See Figure 3.7.)

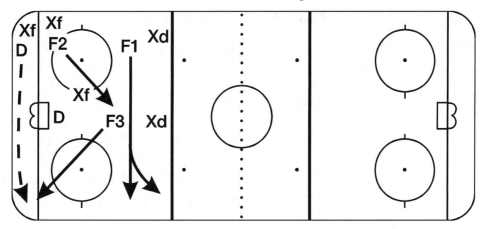

Figure 3.7

Only when the puck carrier has been successfully tied up and/or puck control is gained can the forwards begin to "move" offensively. Although in a defensive posture, offensive options should be considered. The discipline needed to differentiate between these physical and mental factors represents a skill earlier attributed to the likes of Mario Lemieux. In the DZ, movement is not preceded by the assumption that a teammate will get to the puck first. Instead, it is contingent upon the likelihood of puck control itself. Why is this important? Because transitional movements, like those initiated after gaining control of the puck, include leaving your DZ responsibilities in an attempt to get open. This means that the opposition will be left unattended. Thus, "premature" movements run the risk of surrendering potential scoring opportunities should we not gain control of the puck. For example, if our wings are covering the opposition's points, they cannot drop to their normal breakout positions at the hash marks without reading who will first reach the loose puck. When it is evident that we will gain puck control, we can then initiate the transition from defense to offense.

Defensive Zone Coverage: Some Guidelines

Adherence to the principle of "positioning prior to punishment" is required when the rewards accompanying disciplined play begin to manifest. Knowing where everyone is on the ice enables one to move with increased confidence. Remember, do not abandon your zonal responsibilities UNLESS ...

a) ... your assignment floods another zone. In situations involving Xd breaking towards the slot and/or Xf cycling out of the corner, proper DZ coverage calls for staying with your man.

b) ... the puck carrier is successfully being tied up and you can get to the loose puck quickly. Should the D be successful in tying up the puck carrier and you are in position between their nearest support forward and the puck itself, go get it. Prompt retrieval of the puck embodies one of two primary objectives in DZ play — a turnover.

c) ... we have caused a turnover and gain control of the puck. The second objective occurs with the newly acquired puck control, prompting a rapid transition to offense. Accelerated and strategic movements by all involved greatly increase the odds of successfully breaking out of one's own zone.

Because our center may represent the deep man in the OZ (and the last man back), a rotation between himself and the first forward back (weak side wing via the far lane) may be needed so that our center also represents the deep man in the DZ. This rotation must be practiced so that it is quick and efficient. Thus, our wings remain consistently responsible for the opposition's points.

As we already know, the emergence of certain conditions play a crucial role in the proper execution of any defensive system. Overall success is contingent upon the coordination, effort, and discipline of those immediately involved. The principles and expectations derived from basic approaches like those described here, require skills that can be taught, learned, and executed. In short, DZ systems founded on positioning and/or zone play require these 3 basic skills:

1. Discipline - Proper positioning negates mistakes in coverage/running around. "Verbally" mark your man. (Confirms coverage and lessens hesitation.)

2. Patience - Don't chase the puck. Move in straight, direct lines. (No curls/swings.) Force puck movement from the perimeter ... inward.

3. Convergence - Winning battles around the net and along the boards. First man ties up puck carrier. Second man gets to puck before the opposition does.

Teaching Defensive Team Play

Teaching defensive team play, because it consists of a "combination" of man-to-man and zone coverage, should be approached from a "progressive" perspective. Thus, drills designed to exercise specific tactics and movements should gradually increase from basic, to more complex situations (i.e. players rotating in support of teammates' movements). This type of graduation calls for creativity by the coaching staff in designing a successful more "game-like" series of drills exercising the principles at hand. When designing approaches that involve progressive graduations, it is productive to follow these 5 steps:

Step 1. Familiarity and Comfort

Move the puck through the NZ, and into the DZ. Have players react to their zone responsibilities.

Step 2. Isolate Responsibilities

Using a simple drill, add opposition passing within each zone, and eventually from zone to zone. Concentrate on picking up assignments.

Step 3. Generate Continuity

Design increasingly complex drills within each zone separately. Add movement and interchanging of position.

Step 4. Intensify Flow

Design increasingly complex drills moving from zone to zone. Begin in all three zones with simple patterns taken by the opposition. Gradually incorporate interchanging and weaving.

Step 5. Game Conditions

Plan a "controlled" scrimmage aimed at defensive play, emphasizing discipline and execution of tactic goals. Have all players immediately stop on every whistle, in order to correct positional problems.

SECTION II

Offensive Team Play

I had anticipated and prepared for the coming of hockey season, months in advance. The game had taken on a completely different perspective. After all, it would be my first year behind the bench ... rather than on the ice. When I was in my goal crease, I watched the plays in front of me develop and unfold. Because of the angle from which I was permitted to observe, there were times when I knew exactly where the puck was going to be passed — seconds before it actually happened. If I could have only prophesized the same way when the puck was in my own zone.

However, being an ex-goaltender did enhance my knowledge of the game. While at a very young age, coaches had pounded into my somewhat impressionistic head the notion that a goalie is to focus on the puck no matter where it is on the ice. Imagine all that is missed by limiting one's attention to a small vulcanized rubber disk, when there are so many more important things going on which prompt its very movement. Slowly, I began to take my eye off the puck once it was beyond the red line and no longer posed an immediate threat. When this occurred, I would shift my focus to the entire neutral and offensive zones. I became engrossed in the movements of the players, both on offense and defense. The weaving, passing, screening, picking up of assignments, and interchanging of positions were fascinating. During many games, I began to notice particular patterns and systems employed by certain teams and individuals. Between periods, I would draw these up and point them out to my teammates. A longitudinal view allows one to witness the entire play as it unfolds before you. In contrast, the lateral view experienced from the bench is sometimes screened. Although a view of the action from up top is most educational, the goaltender's view can prove quite revealing and helpful to a team.

Yet, I was no longer positioned in that area from which I had studied so many hockey games. Instead, I found myself standing behind a bench. It was now my job to review all the mental and literal notes taken over 22+ years of playing experience, and transfer what I believed were the most appropriate to the particular group of men before me. In such cases, it is imperative to maintain an open mind. Mistakes resulting in modifications and/or adaptations are imminent. Uncontrollable factors such as penalties and injuries require adjustments. Great coaching staffs like those headed by Scotty Bowman and Terry Murray are so prepared, that such adjustments (unless trained to look for it), often go unrecognized throughout the course of a game. Coordinating line rotations and shuffling players around is an art similar to skating, passing, and shooting. Each improves with practice and experience.

During my playing years, I was able to collect and share a wealth of knowledge concerning neutral and offensive zone play. However, play in our defensive zone forced me to narrow my focus on movement of the puck. Looking back, and looking to the present, most forced and unforced turnovers in the DZ can be attributed to a poorly executed transition from defense to offense. This transition, like its counterpart, requires purposeful movement of both bodies and puck. As stated earlier, only when puck control is gained can forwards begin to "move" offensively. Often, successful movement of the puck itself requires a sacrifice from the D or deep support forward. The sacrifice may be manifested in a positional, anaerobic, or physical manner. When deep in our own zone, I often use the analogy of a football quarterback when attempting to translate "what it may take" to get the puck out. Take, for example, a quarterback on a third and long situation. As he looks up from behind the center, he sees that the opposition's secondary has moved into a "blitz" formation. As he takes the snap and drops back into the pocket, he knows what is coming. Yet, the great quarterbacks hang in there until the last possible second. Although they feel and hear the opposing safety as he closes in unblocked, they wait until the intended receiver gets open. Almost, almost, almost ... Now! Here, the quarterback knowingly places himself in a vulnerable position as his arm follows through with the pass, leaving his body off-balance and unprotected. Such individual sacrifices are done for the benefit of the team.

With the puck deep in our DZ, coaches should expect similar sacrifices from players in front of the net and along the boards. Say, for instance, one of our D gain control of the puck deep in the corner with no immediate passing options. Rather than throwing it blindly up the boards with the first sign of pressure, he should move (just as a quarterback scrambles) in attempt to buy the extra second needed by our forwards to get open. Although it means he may take a hit from one of the opposition's forecheckers, he (like the quarterback) must be willing to take that hit in exchange for completing the first crucial pass needed to get the puck out of our zone. Similarly, our forward positioned along the boards must be willing to take a hit from the opposition's pinching Xd, in exchange for taking the time needed to control the puck and pass to the forward curling from the middle in support. The sacrifices needed in the transition from defense to offense usually involve successfully getting the puck out of the DZ, while still maintaining possession. This includes the first element of offensive maneuvering detailed in this book ... or what are otherwise defined as "breakouts."

4

Breaking Out of the Defensive Zone

"Never ascribe to your opponent motives meaner than your own."
— J.M. Barrie, 1922

More often than not, a breakout from the DZ is rushed by one to two forecheckers. This means that little time is allotted for the defense to gain control of the puck while the forwards come back deep in an attempt to get open and receive a pass. In other words, with the exception of the opposition dumping the puck due to a line change or penalty kill situation, successful breakout transitions must be quick, concise, and continually practiced under game-like conditions simulating immediate forechecking pressure.

Movement

Breakouts, as expected, are contingent upon a variety of factors. The most important include the forechecking scheme employed by the opposition and the passing options available as a result of this scheme. Remember, all three forwards should be moving simultaneously ... if not only to support each others' movements, but to act as a decoy. (See Figure 4.1.)

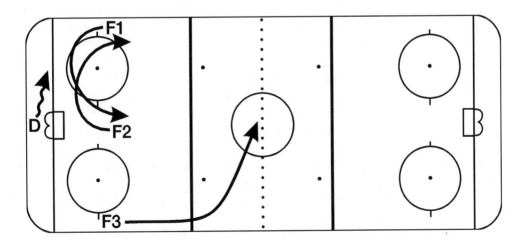

Figure 4.1

Unless an open lane is given, the forwards' movement patterns should assume a rounded or curved path. Skating in straight lines is noticeably less deceptive and easier to defend against. Refer to the options and passing angles created by F1 versus those created by F2.

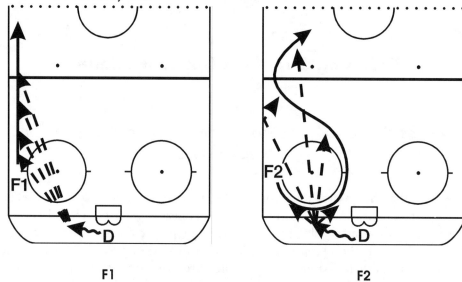

F1   **F2**

Note three obvious benefits from forwards assuming the movement patterns depicted by F1:

1. The passing angle from which F2 must receive the puck is more favorable and thus easier to control.

2. Crossing over allows for acceleration by F2.

3. F2 is not limited to any one lane, but can interchange in a manner more confusing to the opponent's coverage.

It should be emphasized that the players "away" from the puck are just as vital to the success of a breakout. If D1 has the puck, note how his partner can slide to an open area as a reverse or regroup option. In some situations, our wings may need to come back low enough so that the back of the net doesn't obstruct D1's initial pass. Not only will it make these passes easier to handle since the recipient's body already is facing up ice, but also proves more difficult for Xd to pinch against. In other situations, the wings may be forced to turn their back as Xd pinches. Turning your back to the blue line, versus setting up with your back along the side boards, forces Xd to approach from one side — creating room to spin the opposite way. Similarly, duties such as interchanging, screening, and pushing Xd off the blue line are often needed to gain access into the NZ. Quick assessment of the forechecking scheme and immediate execution of proper movements by all five players enhance the likelihood that the DZ will be cleared with puck possession. Consistent achievement of this feat is highly regarded as a "successful transition." The reason this particular aspect of play is emphasized is due to its dual roles within a hockey game. The time it takes to force a turnover, gain control of the puck, and breakout of one's own zone, represents one of the most important phases in a game. The transitional aspect of hockey is not only vital for preventing the opposition from scoring, but also for initiating one's own offensive opportunities.

What to Do, and When to Do It

We can conclude from an earlier discussion on forechecking schemes that most are "adapted" from three basic positional approaches. They include:

    a. 1-man forecheck

    b. 2-man forecheck

    c. NZ Trap

Chances are most forechecking options pitted against you are rooted in one of the above approaches. Teach players to look for these systems, so that appropriate measures and counterpositioning can be taken in order to increase the probability that a successful transition will result. For example, a tight forecheck often forces a breakout pass along the boards. If Xd is instructed, he will pinch in anticipation of the pass. Simple tactics, like taking one to two strides to the middle after receiving the pass, turning your back to Xd, or coming back low enough so that the back of the net doesn't obstruct the first pass, provides the option of banking the puck to a teammate in the NZ by pulling Xd off the boards. Unless facing man-to-man coverage and our puck-controlling D can shake the attacking forechecker, the success of almost every breakout designed, modified, and/or adapted is contingent upon the initial pass being completed and controlled. Successful completion of this first pass is crucial and should be emphasized. Move the puck quickly. Waiting too long increases the angle and difficulty of passes. Sometimes a difficult or mishandled pass may be successfully recovered, but this "luck" eventually runs out. Initial positioning, continued movement towards (or flooding of) a desired area with the goal of opening up passing and skating lanes, combined with the passing and skating itself, are what constitute the recipe required to consistently move the puck beyond the DZ. No matter what side of the ice we attempt to break out, one of our forwards must accelerate through the middle lane, offering immediate support. Similarly, the puck side D should follow his pass and move up with the play as a regroup option.

Game Scenario:

The puck is played deep in our zone, and the opposition sets up their forecheck.

Versus 1-2-2 Tight and/or 1 Man Flush

Because of the tight positioning of the opposition through the extended zones, the first forward back (here, F1) expands his backchecking lane responsibilities to half the ice. Seeing that the opposition will dump the puck strong-side, F1 (after it is apparent that one of our D will reach the puck first) races to a position along the opposite boards. For example, should the puck be dumped into the right corner, F1 will position himself at the hash marks along the left-side boards. D1, knowing that our first forward is coming back via the far lane, immediately wraps the puck around to F1. The primary reason for shifting the breakout to the far side is due to the ice being opened by this particular forecheck. Because all three opposing forwards are positioned puck-side, the reverse, caused by a wrap, forces the entire forechecking unit to shift to an area of ice already occupied by one of our forwards (F1). The movement of teammates supports this first pass, enabling us to overload this area before allowing the opposition to re-establish their forecheck. (See Figure 4.2.)

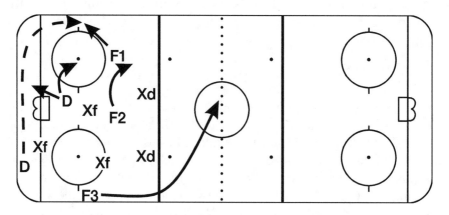

Figure 4.2

D2, making the original pass, spins off his check and heads for the front of the net, while D1 slides into position off the right face-off circle as a potential safety and/or regrouping option for F1. Our second forward back (here, F2) swings with the movement of the puck from right to left and, depending on the positioning of Xd, can do one of two things. If F2 realizes that a 2 on 1 situation can be isolated, he can attempt to force the play by penetrating the NZ in an attempt to draw Xd off the blue line. If Xd stays with F2, F1 may be allowed to walk the puck out of the DZ. However, if it is realized that an aggressive Xd is forcing the play by pinching down low, F2 can anticipate a pass off the boards in the NZ from F1.

The last forward back (F3) fills the far side lane and can assist in the development of a 2 on 1 situation at the blue line by pushing Xd into the NZ. Once there, F3 must determine whether a better passing option is created by remaining wide or cutting to the middle. The D must also realize that their duties do not conclude with a completion of the first pass. Note how the positioning of D1 following the play allows for regrouping or changing the point of attack, should this side of the NZ quickly clog up. (See Figure 4.3.)

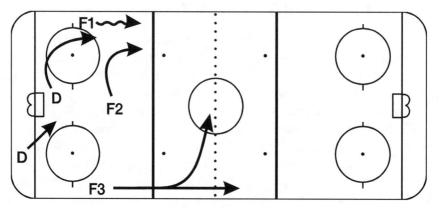

Figure 4.3

Any variations to breakouts designed against this particular forechecking scheme are welcomed. For instance, the initial wrap by D2 can instead be a pass to his defensive partner, assuming position behind the net. Rather than passing to a stationary forward along the boards, either F1 or F2 can swing low out of this corner with momentum. The second forward on this side fills the middle lane. This acceleration with the first pass, rather than after it is completed, makes it difficult for Xd to pinch against two players moving together. (See Figure 4.4.)

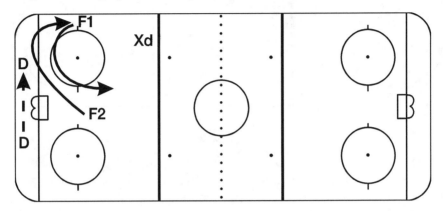

Figure 4.4

No matter how the breakout is modified, success against this particular forechecking scheme shares one key element: Shifting the play to the open side of the ice. Forcing the puck through areas in the DZ overloaded or flooded by the opposition spells "TURNOVER." Reverse the play, and utilize the opposite wing as a breakout option when the opposition's forecheck includes sending three players puck-side.

Versus 1-2-2 (Wide)

This forechecking scheme is both positionally and theoretically different than a tight 1-2-2. The objective of the first forechecker remains to pressure the puck-side D. However, instead of the second and third forecheckers overloading that same area, they maintain their outside lane coverage well into the OZ. The primary intent is to limit our breakout pass through the slot by occupying the wide passing lanes. The positioning of Xd within the middle lanes allows for aggressive movements since the play is going to be forced directly into them.

The most important element needed for success against this forecheck is confidence by the D and F's in handling the puck in and around the slot area. This is accomplished with practice, preparation, and positive encouragement by the coaching staff. Rather than throwing the puck around the boards to an already covered wing, D1 attempts to control by skating behind the net towards the opposite corner (if not pressured) or by passing to his partner dropping behind the net (if pressured). Reversing the play in this manner forces X1 to commit by chasing or curling one way. Our center (F2) must react to the play of D1 and either re-adjust his skating lane to provide a passing option or anticipate the reverse away from the first forechecker. Quick precise movement of both bodies and puck create a man-advantage situation on one side of the ice. (See Figure 4.5.)

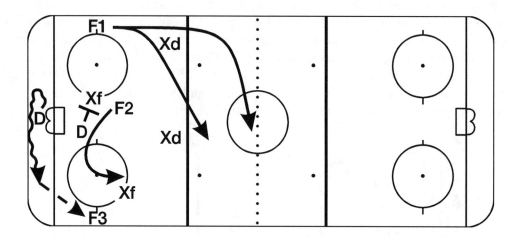

Figure 4.5

Whether the two puck-side forwards interchange or not, the forechecker on that side will be forced to pick up one, leaving the other open. If disciplined, Xf will stay to the outside and force a pass up the middle. Interchanging allows the puck-side wing (F3) to cut to the middle and receive this important pass on his forehand. Should the first forechecker flush D1 behind the net, we may incorporate D2 as a passing option. Although in front of his own net, he is often left unattended. If the forechecker on the opposite side attempts to challenge, the puck can be slid over to a wide open far wing. (See Figure 4.6.)

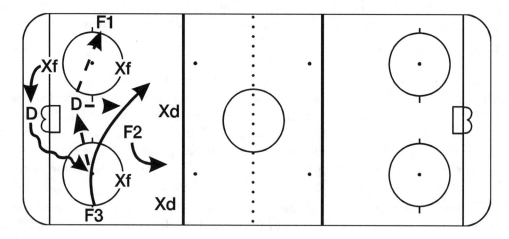

Figure 4.6

Variations of this option are frequently used in powerplay breakouts for the very reason it is successful here. The blue line can be easily gained if we move in a coordinated manner. Movements are designed to get the first forechecker to briefly commit away from the puck. That brief commitment allows us to make the first critical pass by opening up a passing lane to the middle. If your team has control, don't be hesitant to use the D for offensive passing options in order to help create man-advantage situations. Sliding the D off the far post, behind the net, or having them follow up their passes, may represent an important component in the coordination needed to successfully break out. In addition, the forwards must come back deep enough to provide adequate support. Failing to come back to designated depths means that the D will have to force passes to them. There is less likelihood that the puck will be turned over if short, crisp passes are used.

Versus the Neutral Zone Trap

Ah, those 1995 Stanley Cup Champion New Jersey Devils! What was once primarily used in protecting a lead, has been incorporated into an overall defensive scheme ... regardless of score or situation. Coaches like Jacques LeMaire and Roger Nielson have engineered a successful defensive system incorporating this approach. We can all learn from it and can most likely expect to see it some time during our coaching career. Rather than forcing the play deep in the zone, the NZ Trap permits a breakout while flushing the play to one side of the ice. If executed correctly, the puck carrier soon finds himself entering the NZ with limited passing options.

Let's rephrase that last sentence: If executed correctly, the puck carrier finds himself in the NZ with limited options to "headman" the puck. The key to success against the NZ Trap is the ability and confidence to regroup through the extended (defensive) zone. Typically, the puck-carrying D will have room to skate, due to the positioning of the first forechecker in the high slot. D1 can take the given outside lane, however, D2 should drop back rather than remain parallel to the play. After drawing Xf wide, D1 can change the point of attack with a pass back to D2. When this occurs, the Fs regroup accordingly. The wide wing (F3) goes to the boards, with the center (F2) curling as an outlet. The original puck-side wing (F1) cuts to the middle through the NZ. This movement by the forwards at different depths and different angles permits us to gain access to open ice, as well as a man-advantage situation approaching the red line. (See Figure 4.7.)

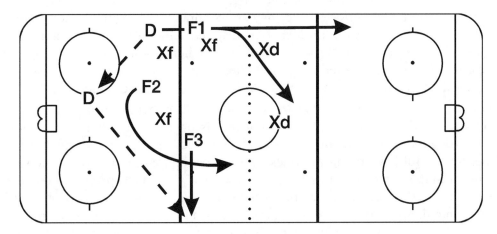

Figure 4.7

Because we have overloaded/flooded one area of the ice with possession of the puck, the opposition is forced to slide. However, the original puck-carrying D remains play high. Look for him to stay wide as both a passing option, or the first man in, should we dump the puck to his side. For example, here we have succeeded in congesting one side of the ice, while still leaving a man free in that far lane. (See Figure 4.8.)

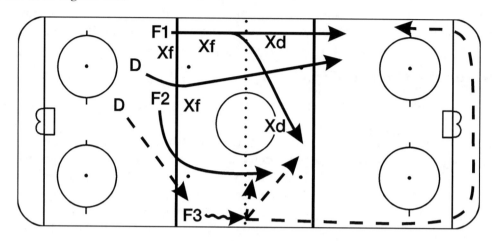

Figure 4.8

Because an increasing number of coaches are looking to 5-man units, it may be necessary to use a D as a deep option from time to time. Such tactics don't comply with the traditional approaches of the past, and Lloyd Percival is probably turning over in his grave. These tactical deviations personify a new game. Today's ice hockey is not the same game it was 15 years ago. European and Soviet principles are continually being fused with North American systems ... and this "fusion" of complementary approaches remains only in its infancy. When was the last time a Stanley Cup winning franchise was led in scoring by a defenseman? How about 1993-94, when the New York Rangers were led in scoring by Sergei Zubov. With every game watched, I saw something and/or took notes on some new technique. Systems including regrouping, interchanging, and acceleration & deceleration tactics are far from being perfected and they are continually changing. In accordance, the role of the D have taken on increased responsibility. Defensive pairings often require at least one to quarterback the offense, when not attending to defensive duties. Just as football quarterbacks must sometimes carry the ball and engage the opposition, the D in today's hockey are being asked to do the same.

Referring to Figure 4.8, whether we attempt to utilize this D, or have him immediately headman the puck while breaking out, is up to the coaching staff. Either way, shifting the play back and across to D2, often leaves this original puck carrier alone. Successfully wrapping the puck around, or dumping it into this far corner, can result in this same player beating an opponent who has to pivot and come all the way across the ice. Tactical maneuvers such as 4-man rushes which instruct a D to jump into the play, have added a new dimension to the game. However, remember to instruct players that whenever a D is given the green light to carry the puck out of the DZ and/or penetrate deep in the OZ, the high forward on that side must drop back in support. When employing the 5-man unit approach, players must learn to move in accordance with one another. Communication and coordination are the keys to success. Coaches that are more comfortable with a conservative role assumed by the D can initiate a breakout against this forecheck with the first forward back-swinging behind the net to pick up the puck. As stated, coordinated movement typically enables the initial puck carrier unrestricted access into the NZ and beyond. (See Figure 4.9.)

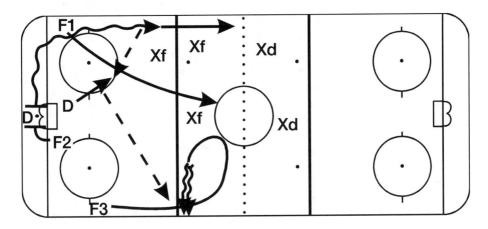

Figure 4.9

Game Scenario:

The puck is played deep in our zone, and the opposition forechecks aggressively.

Versus 2-Man Flush

"If we're inside the OZ and you don't see the logo on the opponent's jersey, the first two forwards have the green light to pressure hard." The message conveyed by this phrase is somewhat universal among most coaches. I remember hearing it at least once a game. Simply put, if only the name and/or number of the opposing defenseman's jersey is visible to the forecheckers once inside the blue line, he cannot be facing the play, nor has he been able to analyze his passing options. Therefore, two forecheckers may be instructed to pressure and force the play. This is an obviously much more aggressive approach to forechecking.

What movements by our Fs and D increase the odds of breaking the puck out against this pressure? Again, the most critical aspect of a successful breakout against any 2-man forecheck is the initial pass. In most cases, the puck carrier will be flushed deep in his own zone, behind the net, and into the oncoming second forechecker. Compare this to a quarterback holding on to the ball until the last second. Although the D may feel pressure, they must suck both forecheckers as deep as possible and give their forwards the time needed to get open. In most cases, they should be prepared to trade a hit behind the net for a successful first breakout pass. Because it is a 2-1-2, the third forechecker will attempt to take away any passing lanes up the middle. In addition, the Xd will anticipate passes being thrown around the boards and look to pinch. Should one of our teammates yell "Two men!", anticipate a quick transition attempting to trap two Xf down low.

Skating behind the net with two forecheckers converging, the puck carrier has two options: The first involves the far-side wing coming across the ice. If D1 is playing his correct side, he should be able to wrap a strong forehand reverse back to the wing (F1) which he is skating away from. F1 must have come back low enough so that the Xd on that side does not have the opportunity to pinch. Although he may originally set up high along the boards as a decoy, once D1 is about to reverse the puck, F1 must quickly move down to a lower area. The far side wing (F3) is not covered at this point and can quickly swing towards F1 as an outlet. Note the increased ease of this pass with both wings on their forehand. The movement of the center (F2) is critical in drawing the third forechecker away from the play. Because the path of F2 is adjacent with the original movement of D1 to the opposite corner, the third forechecker will most likely drift with him to that side of the ice. By the time it is realized that the far-side wing is the primary option, that forechecker will have been lured out of the play with his teammates caught in deep. (See Figure 4.10.)

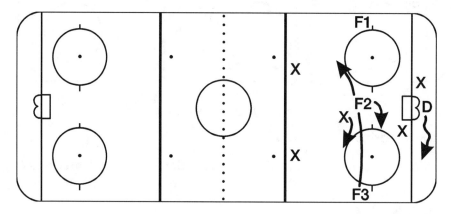

Figure 4.10

If the third forechecker should eventually begin to pick up the far-side wing coming across, then F2 remains alone and heads towards an open area of ice. By communicating (i.e. instructions from the goaltender or defensive partner), D1 can look to wrap the puck to F2 in the opposite corner rather than reversing the play. F3 continues with his momentum to the outside, and F1 comes off the boards in an attempt to fill the vacant middle lane. (See Figure 4.11.)

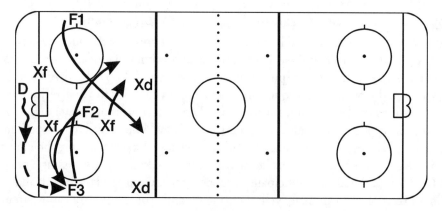

Figure 4.11

The second option available against two oncoming forecheckers is similar to the first. Instead of reversing, D1 wraps a pass to the wing which he is skating towards. Again, this wing must position himself low enough to provide time against an aggressive Xd. This type of wrap, because it is really a pass, may need to be practiced for two specific reasons. First, the puck must beat at least one oncoming forechecker. Second, it is critical that the forwards can immediately handle these types of passes. Remember, pressure may be felt quickly from either Xd or Xf. Rather than the opposite wing coming across, F2 stays parallel to the path taken by D1 around the net. Upon receiving the puck along the boards, F1 can deflect a short pass to F2 accelerating through the middle lane. This is best accomplished when F1 feels immediate pressure from the points. However, should F1 have time to better control the puck (due to poor anticipation or execution by the opposition), he can interchange with F2. Here, the forward swinging to the outside cuts in front of the puck carrier, in order that we may use him to: a) screen Xd if needed; or, b) use as a wide passing option should Xd drift to the middle. The wing on the opposite side (F3) can remain wide, cut behind the middle Xd and come across, or cut in front of Xd, in attempt to split the opposition's defense. His movement depends upon the cushion given. (See Figure 4.12.)

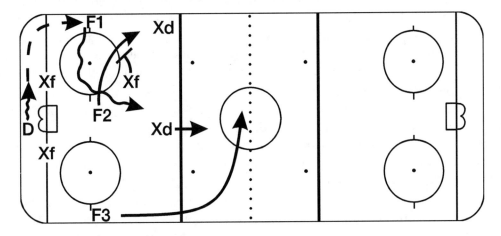

Figure 4.12

Introducing these two options poses little difficulty due to the consistency of the wing's positioning. Regardless of the scenario, both set up near the boards. It is imperative that everyone watch the play of D1. F2 swings parallel with the original flow; however, the wing on this side must anticipate the possibility of a reverse. Should this occur, the far-side wing must quickly react by coming across as a passing outlet. It also may prove wise for the forwards to "think ahead" and base their actions on the "shot" of D1. For instance, note the difference in accuracy and speed of a pass made from the forehand versus the backhand while being pressured. Thus, should D1 pick up the puck on his forehand, it might prove easier to continue along this line and make the pass towards the wing being approached (provided he is open). Similarly, D1 picking the puck up on his backhand might put more velocity on the pass by reversing it, again using his forehand.

Immediately after controlling a puck along the boards, look to utilize the middle lane if given. Passing the puck to a forward accelerating through this lane often forces the Xd to relinquish the blue line. Should Xd decide to step up, the NZ is opened for the wing coming across. It's amazing what can happen when you force opposing Xd to make such split-second decisions. Variables such as hesitation, and/ or the time needed to mentally process an immediate situation, often result in mistakes. If your team knows what to do and when to do it, you will gain a tremendous advantage.

Rapid Counterattacks

> *"Quick speed is good, where wisdom leads the way."*
> *— Robert Green, Selimus, 1594*

In short, wisdom both develops and facilitates speed. Knowing immediately what to do and when to do it is manifested via swift, precise movement. If team "A" is spontaneous in their movement whereas team "B" has to continually stop and think, which team controls the flow? The elapsed time required to mentally encode, process, and retrieve a specific scenario may be all that is needed to place one team over another. For this reason, quick transition drills need to be designed and incorporated into practices. However, as the quote which precedes this section suggests, the success of spontaneity is contingent upon knowledge. Thus, educational techniques such as diagramming, discussing, and walking through plays (both on and off the ice) can prove extremely beneficial when teaching such movements.

Examples of these quick movements often occur in the transition from defense to offense, otherwise known as "rapid counterattacks" (RCats). If the opposition is forced to relinquish puck control via a dump or turnover, our forwards must immediately switch responsibilities from defensive coverage ... to offensive breakout. Depending on the positioning of the opposing players, a quick RCat may prove more prosperous than a set breakout.

For instance, if it is noticed that all three Xf are continually drawn to one side of the ice while forechecking, we can explore the option of setting up our far wing (F3) wide. One way to accomplish this is by disguising a cross-ice pass with normal breakout skating patterns. (See Figure 4.13.)

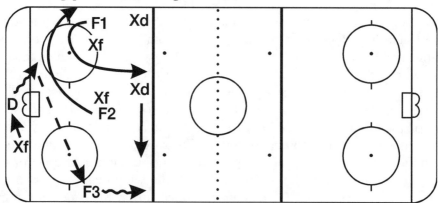

Figure 4.13

A variation curls F2 toward the puck-carrying wing (F1), in attempts to push Xd off the blue line by skating towards the seam between them. F3 remains wide and should not yet accelerate towards the NZ. If Xd plays this option and is pushed off the blue line, F2 allows a "forceful" pass from F1 through to F3 on the far wing. Should the Xd on the point elect to pinch, F1 can slide the puck beyond him towards the two forwards in the NZ. Of course, the puck must get safely beyond the extended zone. (See Figure 4.14.)

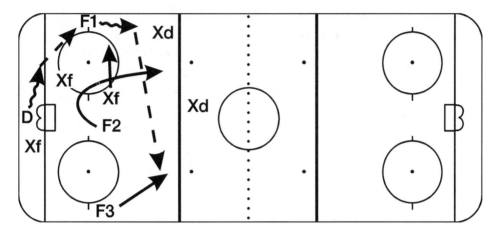

Figure 4.14

Should the coaching staff note Xd playing "too-aggressive" on the points, examine the middle lane as a passing option. By playing overly aggressive, Xd continually look to pinch. Hence, the gap between them begins to widen. This is especially true with younger, less experienced defensemen. Breaking both wings (F1 and F3) wide forces Xd to stay wide. Here, F2 curls in the DZ and screens one Xd off the puck. At the blue line, one (or both) of the wings abruptly cut to the middle looking for a long breakout pass. As with most breakouts, the D must keep in mind that his pass may have to beat at least one Xf. For this reason, such passes must be practiced. (See Figure 4.15.)

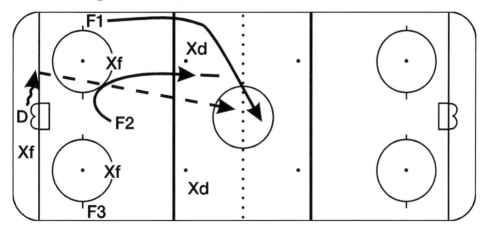

Figure 4.15

Additional scenarios where the design of rapid counterattacks may prove productive involve the following:

a. X shoots wide, and our D is in closest proximity of the puck. Because the momentum of the opposition will be "incoming," look to send our weak-side wing into the NZ against this flow.

b. A delayed change. Following a dump-in (with both teams changing lines), send only two forwards back into the DZ. If the opposing unit skates past our bench, slide F1 off the bench behind Xd.

c. Two Xf get caught deep and/or Xd unsuccessfully pinches. If we complete the first pass, look for D2 (in front of the net) to jump into the play.

Breaking Out of the Defensive Zone: A Summary

1) Successful completion of the first pass is often crucial.

2) The entire on-ice unit must move with a purpose and in support of each other.

3) Only after puck control has been gained can we "move" offensively.

Versus 1-2-2 Tight/Flush: Shift play to open ice by utilizing far wing.

Versus 1-2-2 Wide: F2 anticipates and curls with reverse, producing a man-advantage situation on one side of the ice.

Versus NZ Trap: Change the point of attack by regrouping in the DZ.

Versus 2-1-2 Flush: First pass must beat at least one oncoming forechecker. Support "times" his movement towards the receiving forward.

Rapid Counterattacks involve quick transitional movements following dumps or turnovers by the opposition. They often include positional tactics designed to gain immediate access into the NZ and beyond. Such movements may involve long and/or indirect passes, which need to be continually practiced. Indirect passes are those banked off the boards, glass, or lead passes played to open ice in anticipation of a teammate.

If no passing/skating options exist, fire the puck "high" off the glass, and into the NZ. Better to make X clear the zone and regroup than risk a DZ turnover.

5

Moving through the Neutral Zone

"Skill and Confidence are an unconquered army."
- George Herbert, Jacula Prudentum

The Overlooked Neutral Zone

Viewed by many as the most "overlooked" and negated of the three zones coached, the NZ often plays a vital role in whether offense or defense needs to be assumed. I welcome all coaches to review the tapes from their last game and count the number of both forced and unforced turnovers occurring in the NZ. How many of these turnovers helped produce a scoring opportunity either for your own team or the opposition? It's not uncommon for this number to exceed a half dozen per game — per team. Success or failure in this zone can lead to a significant number of scoring chances gained or forfeited. Since the previous section defined our roles within a transitory phase, let us now begin to examine what options exist should we move beyond the DZ with definite possession of the puck.

Game Scenario:

Following a successful breakout, we penetrate the NZ with puck control.

Neutral Zone Rushes (Man-Advantage Situation)

The first of these options involve the development of a "rush" towards the OZ. The most obvious scenario exists as a man-advantage situation (3 on 2, 2 on 1, etc.). To confuse the backcheckers and opposing Xd, encourage the forwards to attempt "at least" one interchange. In other words, have two (or more) of the rushing forwards change lanes. It is not uncommon for the third forward to remain wide, in an attempt to spread out the opposition. (See Figure 5.1.)

In fact, most rushes through the NZ are designed to produce a man-advantage situation in a "workable" area of ice. For example, if our puck-side D should jump into a previous 3 on 3 rush, a simultaneous wide pullout lane taken by the far wing (F3) forces that particular backchecker to stay with him. Hence, we now have created a 3 on 2 situation on one side of the ice. This is commonly referred to as "stretching" the opposition while "overloading" a particular area or lane. (See Figure 5.2.)

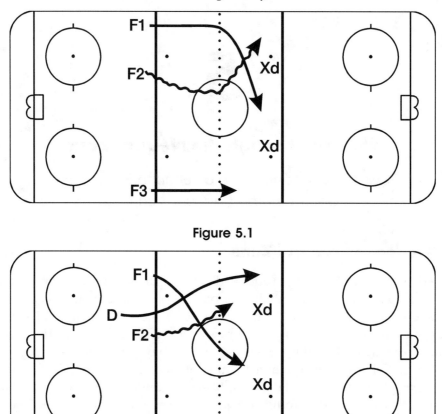

Figure 5.1

Figure 5.2

The movement by all involved must be coordinated and quick. In addition to the interchanging and overloading, many advanced level coaches also incorporate the principle of "Deceleration and Acceleration" when approaching their opponent's blue line. This principle, referred to as "D & A," has existed within the syllabus of European coaches for years. It is believed to have been developed by Anatoli Tarasov while coaching the great Soviet Red Army Teams of the 1970's and 80's. The D & A principle is as follows: While approaching the opposition's Xd in the NZ, the puck carrier purposely decelerates, causing Xd to decelerate. Xd may even be instructed to "step up" in these situations, in an attempt not to surrender the blue line. Simultaneously, the support options accelerate in anticipation of a pass, or if not open, a dump retrieval. These support options exist as the interchanging of forwards, or the addition of a defenseman assuming an offensive role. Notice how the timing of this acceleration is "prior" to receiving a pass, rather than "after" the pass has been made. If practiced consistently and correctly, the passing needed to address these quick spurts of speed will enhance most offenses. The puck-receiving player moves faster than Xd at the point of confrontation as a result of the D & A principle. (See Figures 5.3a and 5.3b.)

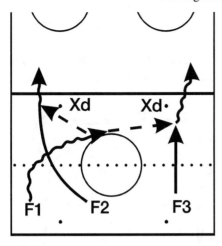

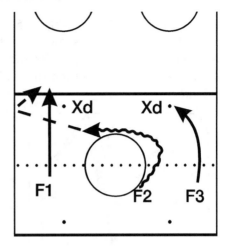

Figure 5.3a   Figure 5.3b

Dump and Chase (Man-Disadvantage Situation)

The second option, should puck possession be maintained in the NZ, is the dump and chase. However, this option need not require relinquishing puck control. Although the literal definition of the word "dump" denotes "an unloading or discarding," it encompasses only the initial phase of our intention. With the exception of a line change or penalty kill situation, dumping the puck in the OZ is an offensive tactic. Scouting reports that pin-point a weaker or less experienced Xd, may result in a game plan which includes continually dumping the puck into this particular corner. The immediate pressure received from (at least) one forechecker, as well as the support positioning of those eliminating potential breakout options, may force Xd to mishandle the puck and/or make an errant pass. The result is an OZ turnover, with our forwards already knowing where to position themselves around the net. Although not a transition to offense, certain responsibilities assumed between when the puck was "controlled" versus "recontrolled," are necessary should our goal be to crash the net ... with possession.

Should the unit on the ice need to be replaced due to fatigue, instruct players to dump the puck bench-side. This accomplishes two things: First, the fatigued and refreshed players can be exchanged more quickly. Second, rather than furnishing an open far lane, Xd is now forced to make a cross-ice pass in order to break out from their own zone. Long passes such as these are typically less accurate and more difficult to control by moving players.

However, dumping the puck with the intention to chase and regain control is often the result of a man-disadvantage situation. Unsupported in the NZ with a backchecker and/or Xd about to converge upon him, the puck carrier dumps deep into the OZ. Here, just as we call upon our D when breaking out, the puck carrier may need to buy an extra second awaiting support. The phrase "ragging the puck" has been affixed to this tactic. Again, the D & A principle can be exercised. By decelerating, F1 causes Xd to do the same. Cutting to the middle, the puck is dumped cross corner. (See Figure 5.4a.) If cutting to the outside, the puck can be wrapped to the far side (See Figure 5.4b.) Note how the support options accelerating through the NZ now assume the potential of beating Xd to the puck. Where Xd still has to pivot and accelerate, F2 and/or F3 are already skating at top speed. Even if Xd does reach the puck first, he will be immediately pressured by one or two forecheckers.

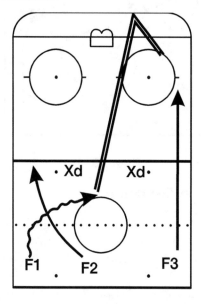

Figure 5.4a

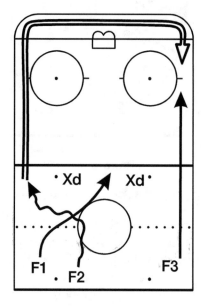

Figure 5.4b

First and foremost, every time we dump the puck ... we must get it deep. As will be discussed with more detail in later chapters diagramming OZ strategies, the first man in retrieves the puck. The second man in can either drive to the net or offer support down low (i.e., in the corner or behind the net). The third man in approaches the high slot as a "second wave" attacker, and reacts to the puck movement initiated by his teammates.

Thus, unsupported and on "their" side of the red line, we can expect the puck carrier to dump and give chase. But what if the puck is still on "our" side of the red line? As was introduced in Chapter 4 on breakouts, there exists an option other than forcing penetration at a man-disadvantage (NZ turnover) or "icing" the puck (DZ face-off). If unsupported and still on "our" side of the red line, look to regroup and change the point of attack.

Regrouping in the Neutral Zone

The third option available within the NZ is the "regroup." This option is based on the principle that puck control should not be surrendered voluntarily. Should neither an open lane to penetrate the OZ (perpetuating a rush), nor time for the support forwards to accelerate through the NZ (setting up a D & A scenario designed to elicit either a continued rush or dump play) exist, teach players not to be intimidated in reverting the play in an attempt to re-organize the attack. Obviously, a "good look" precedes any pass made in the direction towards one's own goal.

In most scenarios involving backchecking, the first two forwards back will head towards the outside lanes. As was mentioned earlier, both the D and last forward back are responsible for the middle lanes. However, note the gap that may develop between these players should the D follow up the play correctly. (See Figure 5.5.)

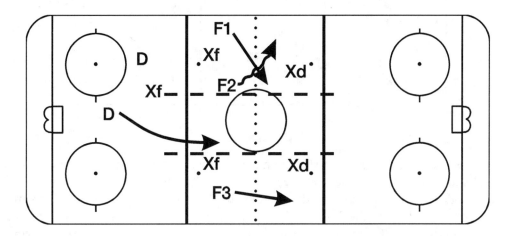

Figure 5.5

If our D play as they are coached, they will remember that when on offense "play within the same zone as the puck." However, both D do not remain parallel to each other with puck control. By playing at different depths, or what is called "staggered," cross-ice passes do not have to be forced through traffic. Their duties do not cease with a successful first breakout pass, but include moving up with the play as it perforates the NZ. In fact, at least one D needs to continually maintain position as a passing option in all three zones. The gap sometimes created by players breaking through the NZ permits those mobile D, who abide with the rush, to be utilized in the option of regrouping. It is often the ability of the D to initiate the breakout, shake off the forechecker(s), and hustle up to the NZ which determines whether this option exists. The objective of passing the puck back when regrouping is to allow our forwards the opportunity to reorganize the attack while accelerating through this zone.

As previously noted, the middle lanes are sometimes vacated and can be used to our advantage in this situation. For instance, a pass reverted back to our D may capture and sustain the attention of the opposing forwards, while simultaneously allowing our forwards to change lanes and pick up speed. Even if just for a second, their middle lane forechecker may hesitate in deciding whether to pick up one of our forwards — or pressure our D. Should the D receiving the pass intentionally skate so as to lure a crowd towards one side of the ice, disciplined movements by his teammates result in a man-advantage situation in another lane or area. (See Figure 5.6.)

This strategy is referred to by most coaches as changing the point of attack. Note here, how the movement of F2 (with the puck) draws at least two forecheckers. As mentioned earlier, D2 does not remain parallel with the play, but assumes the more

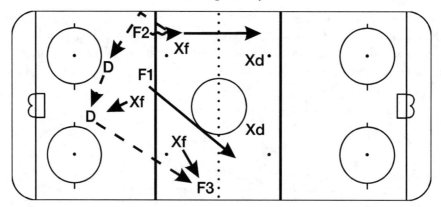

Figure 5.6

disciplined role of providing the outlet from which the direction of the original attack is altered. The far side wing (F3) must also be disciplined and maintain his wide positioning. As the pass travels from D1 to D2 to F3, the opposition's forwards will most likely follow the lateral movement of the puck across the ice. This increases the difficulty for the opposition to turn, find, and catch one of our players. Because most will look to stay with their nearest check, the opposing forward responsible for F2 will often look to stay with him. Similarly, their deep forechecker will most likely pressure our D. The movement of our players should take this into account. Here, the right Xd is forced to remain wide due to F2 breaking down the far lane. As a result of the interchanging of F1 and F2, we open up the middle lane and create a man-advantage situation in a workable area of ice. If F3 can neither carry the puck, nor feed F1 coming through the middle, he has the option of wrapping to F2 accelerating down the opposite wing.

   In addition to using this tactic when regrouping in the NZ, changing the point of attack has been quite effective when breaking out against the forecheck of a NZ Trap. The main difference being that D1 may be flushed to one side by the first forechecker well before reaching the blue line. In fact, the initial pass from D1 to D2 may occur within one's own slot. However, because the first forechecker in a NZ Trap is neither aggressive nor supported, the first pass is not regarded as very dangerous. (See Figure 5.7.)

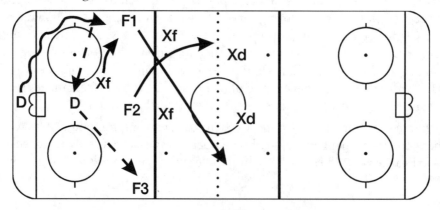

Figure 5.7

A second popular design within regrouping stems from the strategic placement of one forward against the boards, while the other two curl and accelerate through the NZ. As with any pass to a stationary forward, there must be moving support. Here all three forwards curl back towards D1 and D2, but neither on the same or depth. Remember that lateral puck movement needs to be followed by a quick headman (or "quick up"). Waiting too long increases the difficulty of passes and gives X the opportunity to position themselves. (See Figure 5.8.)

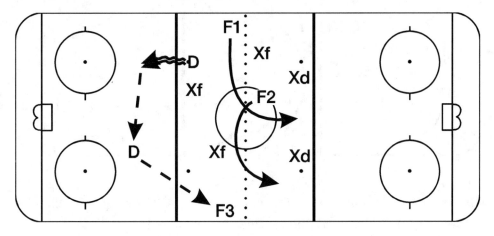

Figure 5.8

The first pass from D1 to D2 is vital because it initiates the flow of the re-organized attack. Note how the gap existing in the middle lanes is exploited here. The interchanging of F2 and F3 on different lines and at different depths forces the opposing forward to choose an assignment. Again, our movements have created a man-advantage situation within a workable area of ice. Depending on the recourse taken by Xf, D2 can:

a. headman to F2 accelerating up the wing, or

b. headman to F3 accelerating to the middle. (See Figure 5.9.)

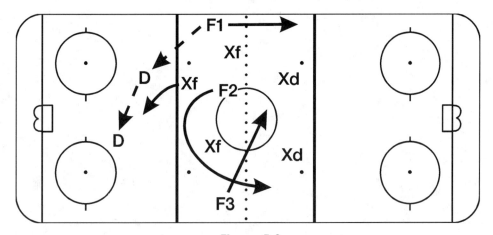

Figure 5.9

In either scenario, F1 fulfills his task of taking both the backchecking forward and right Xd deep to the net. This permits D1 to jump into the play by opening up the extended zone on that same side.

In addition to regroups designed with one forward immediately going to the boards (as previously described), many coaches recognize options which include the interchanging of both wings. (See Figure 5.10.)

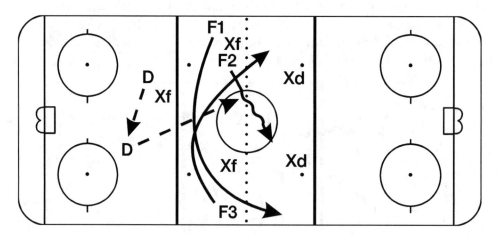

Figure 5.10

The advantages of going D1 to D2 while the wings interchange are threefold:

a. Once again, the vacated middle lanes are exploited.

b. Unless specifically instructed, the backchecking forwards are typically confused as to when/if they should leave their original assignments and pick up the forward coming across. This confusion and hesitation often leads to mistakes in coverage.

c. Should we penetrate the OZ, the coaching staff can design plays towards the net utilizing the fact that both wings are now on their "off" side. Because one-timers prove quite difficult for goaltenders to stop and control, teach players to aggressively crash the net for rebounds.

Neutral Zone Offense: A Summary

Includes puck movement following a successful breakout or rapid counterattack resulting from a turnover.

Keep in mind, most breakouts will be the result of work along the boards. Once in the NZ, look to move the puck into the middle. This creates more options as we approach the OZ.

Deceleration and Acceleration Principle (D & A):

This principle demonstrates that Xd will often decelerate in an attempt to remain in consistent proximity should the puck carrier decelerate and/or abruptly cut to the middle or outside lanes. Conversely, the support options should immediately accelerate. A successful pass to one of these teammates will result in the intended receiver moving faster than Xd at the point of confrontation. This principle can be applied within each of the options below.

NZ Rush — Man Advantage Situation

Should include at least one interchange of those involved to confuse both the opposing defensemen and backcheckers. Communicate. If a teammate fills your lane, you fill their lane.

Dump & Chase — Man-Disadvantage Situation

Design player movements with the goal of regaining puck control and creating offensive opportunities.

Regrouping — No Existing Headman Lanes

Attempt to re-organize the attack by playing the puck back to the defense, with forwards interchanging and accelerating through NZ.

- If unsupported and on "their" side of the red line ... look to dump and chase.
- If unsupported and on "our" side of the red line ... look to regroup.

Defensive Transition:

If we lose control of the puck, our middle lane/high forward immediately positions himself between Xd in an attempt to take away their regroup option. By limiting puck movement to a smaller, less workable area of ice, we make it easier to defend against.

6

Attacking in the Offensive Zone

"There is always more spirit in the attack, than in the defense."
- Livy, Histories, XXI

All the information and strategy that has been discussed thus far, concludes with the same final goal. That is to say forechecking, backchecking, breaking out, and moving the puck through the NZ are all designed and implemented to enhance the opportunity of access into the OZ. Indeed, offense can be recruited. However, individual skills cannot carry a team very far in today's game of ice hockey. In a one on one situation, the more talented offensive player will succeed in achieving better scoring opportunities. But it may be the culmination of his teammates' forechecking and/or passing which created the opportunities.

While on a bus ride to some small town en route to play a minor league game, I listened as my coach shared a story with a young player who had just been acquired by our club. He talked of his days playing in the NHL and the importance of roles assumed by various players. Although some roles may be prettier than others, success is contingent upon the fulfillment of each. It was conceded that, like many organizations, there existed one or two lines which were considered the "go to" lines. A large percentage of the offense was contributed by the forwards which comprised these lines. Often, they were double-shifted to match up against weaker opposing units, and their skills called upon during powerplay opportunities. Although no names were mentioned, he recalled one particular line which worked as well as any he had ever seen. Evidently, two of the three forwards finished the season among the top five scorers in the entire league. The third forward assumed more of a "power" role, and although working well with the others, he failed to put up the same numbers. Postseason discussions in the locker room centered on recognition. Team MVP was considered a highly coveted award. Not only did it bring a great amount of prestige to one's name, it was a nice addition to the resume as ammunition during contract negotiations. Almost everyone agreed that one of the top two leading scorers would be awarded the honor. Some were even wagering money on which player would win. However, unbeknownst to all, the two players in question met with the coaching staff to recommend that the honor be awarded to the third linemate. As the story unfolded, the message became clear. Indeed, this line was comprised of at least two offensive talents who could pick any corner at will and deke a goaltender out of his suspenders. Yet, they too acknowledged that their success would not have been without someone digging pucks out of the corners and feeding them in front. Whether the account is fact or fiction remains irrelevant. Success in the OZ, as well as everywhere on the ice, requires individual efforts ... but as a unit.

With respect to the obvious features stressed in the aforementioned tale, this chapter will emphasize two similar areas of offensive play. The first will follow the progressive flow from NZ to OZ. Here, foundations of various strategies used in attacking the opposition's zone, as well as penetrating the high slot, will be detailed. Should puck control occur deep in the OZ, the second section of this chapter will focus on attacking the net from this area.

Offensive Zone Attacks

For a discussion on offensive attacks, let us assume that our movement through the NZ has been successful ... and we have penetrated the OZ while maintaining puck control. The puck carrier must immediately realize the options which exist before him. If the blue line is given, will support be received by cutting to the middle or outside lanes? Will it prove more beneficial to dump or wrap the puck to an accelerating teammate? Should he attempt to stickhandle around Xd, or play it safe and dump now that the extended zone has been gained?

An overriding theme throughout the defensive sections of this book has focused on the power of positioning prior to punishment. From an offensive perspective, positioning precedes and promotes potential ... that is scoring potential. Such potential is drawn from the ability to create man-advantage situations and/or win individual battles. Many breakout and regrouping drills often result in odd man rushes. Similarly, a review of most breakout and regrouping game strategies are designed with similar goals in mind. For these reasons, penetration into the OZ via a man-advantage situation (2 on 1, 3 on 2) will be emphasized. One of the most critical factors in such rushes is the positioning of those involved. In 3-man rushes, the concept of "triangulation" has proven very effective. Note how the puck carrier attempts to draw one Xd, leaving a man-advantage situation in front of the net. Passing options are created by F1 and F3 playing at different depths. For example, the gap created by F1 remaining high in the middle slot and F3 going to the net causes the second Xd to choose coverage between the two. (See Figure 6.1.)

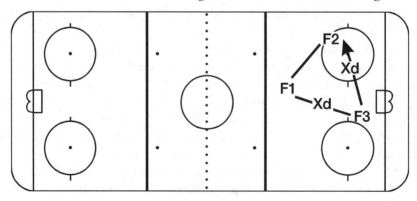

Figure 6.1

Tactics such as this can promote quality shot opportunities. However, even before attempting to triangulate, other factors must be considered. Should we gain the blue line in the OZ, our forwards must immediately recognize the location on the ice from which they are attacking ... as well as their options. Does the puck carrier occupy the middle or outside lanes? This can be an important determinant in the ensuing movements of the support forwards. Opinions differ as to what path/lane ought to be taken by the puck carrier. These opinions are based on two different theories. Although undefined, they exist as the middle lane and outside lane attacks.

Attacking from the Middle Lane: Triangulation

A. Some coaches will instruct the puck carrier (F2) to penetrate the middle lane (if given), when attempting to gain access into the OZ. By design, several options become immediately available. The motivation behind this strategy is the movement "imposed onto" Xd. At some point, one of the opposing defenseman must either step up and/or pivot to the middle in order to play the puck carrier. If the middle is being controlled, wide positioning of the support forwards (F1 and F3) immediately opens an unprotected passing lane when Xd is forced to step up and play F2. (See Figure 6.2.)

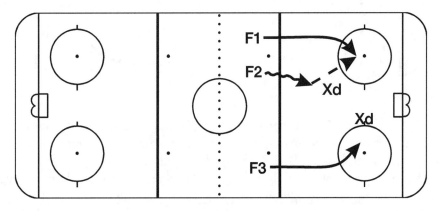

Figure 6.2

A.1 If sufficient time is available (i.e. no backchecking pressure), a variation of this option entails the puck carrier (F2) to suddenly stop in the high slot and play Xd's response. Again, whichever Xd steps up, the support forward on that side immediately becomes open. Should both Xd continue to back in, F2 can put a high quality shot on net, with two forwards already converging for a rebound. (See Figure 6.3.)

B. Should the puck carrier (F2) gain access from the outside lane and cut towards the middle, a simple interchange with the forward on that side produces a similar situation. Here, F2 holds on to the puck, causing Xd to pivot towards the middle. (See Figure 6.4.)

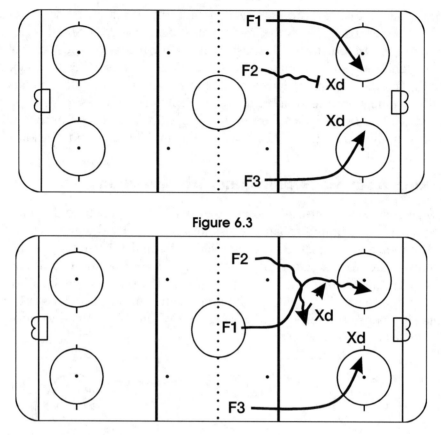

Figure 6.3

Figure 6.4

In this case, a "sharp" interchange by both F2 and F1 causes Xd to hesitate due to the quick directional changes involved with following the movement of each. The sudden quickness and sharp angles involved should continually be practiced. Movements of this type cause confusion among defensemen in choosing coverage.

C. Should the puck carrier (F2) already occupy the middle lane with his momentum taking him wide, a drop pass left for the forward interchanging in support of his movement (F1), once again results in a middle lane attack. (See Figure 6.5.)

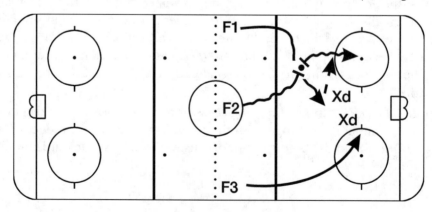

Figure 6.5

Note the consistency in the "triangular" approach created by these movements. At some point, Xd will be forced to step up and play the puck carrier now penetrating the high slot.

D. If we find ourselves in a position where one of the D is forced into joining the attack (i.e. in need of goals), further adaptations can be incorporated into our confrontation with Xd. However, with D1 offering offensive support, F2 may need to modify his positioning. (See Figure 6.6.)

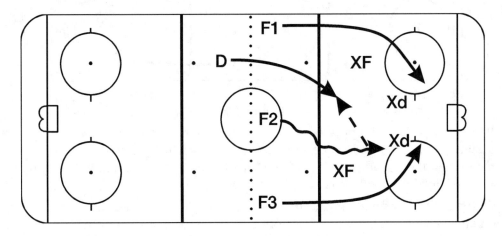

Figure 6.6

If designing such movements for your players, keep in mind that roles can be productively altered — without altering the objective.

Following penetration into the OZ, our far-side forward can attempt to break wide and deep in an attempt to draw the Xd on that side with him. In fact, the movements of all can provide several different scenarios. Should those players assuming the support roles exist as the respective wingers, both remain on their forehand and can be expected to better handle sharp angle passes. However, if interchanging results in the unprotected forward playing on his off-side, practice setting up and shooting one-timers with the opposite forward crashing the net.

Attacking From the Outside Lane: Isolation

Isolation — Similar to those quarterbacked from the middle lane, offensive attacks directed from the outside attempt to get at least one Xd to commit by pivoting and/or stepping up. However, rather than looking to headman the puck, the primary objective is to feed back to the middle — or across to the opposite forward. If the movements of all three players are in conjunction with one another, attacking from an outside lane should permit a man-advantage situation versus one Xd. That is to say, if the opposite forward is successful in taking Xd wide and deep (to the far post), we have "isolated" a 2 on 1 advancing towards the net. (Figure 6.7.)

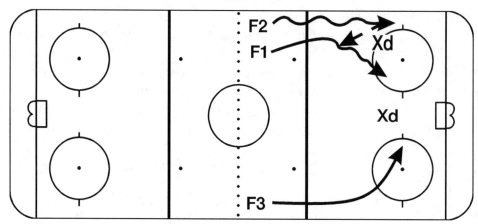

Figure 6.7

If left unprotected, F3 now becomes a primary target, breaking towards the slot and still on his forehand. Note how designs, which instruct the puck carrier to penetrate via the outside lanes, typically involve movements intended to draw Xd from in front of the net.

A. If the OZ is gained via the middle lane, and it is realized that a particularly inexperienced or weaker Xd is positioned to one side, allow the puck carrier (F2) to exploit this situation. Should F2 keep the puck while pursuing an outside lane, this should immediately be recognized as a cue dictating the subsequent movement of his support forwards. The opposite forward (F3) now knows to break for the far post, in an attempt to draw Xd with him. The forward, which has assumed the high slot (F1) vacated by the puck carrier, will attempt to play the situation as a 2 on 1. (See Figure 6.8.)

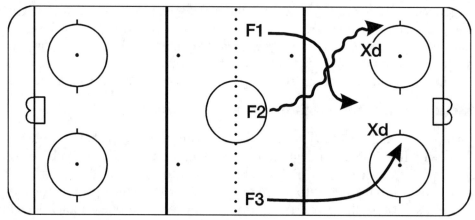

Figure 6.8

B. If the OZ is instead gained via an outside lane, the puck carrier's (F1) movement towards the middle signifies to the forward occupying that lane (F2) to cut behind him, enabling the successful completion of a drop pass. Hence, we have created the same scenario as described above. (See Figure 6.9.)

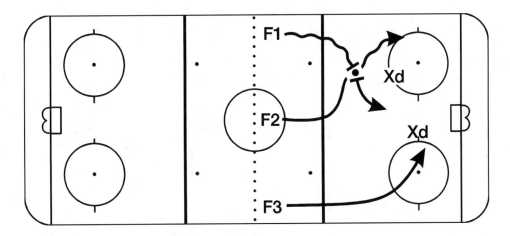

Figure 6.9

C. We have all witnessed the great Denis Savard in action. When penetrating the OZ, he is one of the most exciting players to watch ... simply because we anticipate the creation of a scoring opportunity. One of his playing trademarks includes the "spin-o-rama." Even though he successfully uses this move everywhere on the ice, it has proven especially productive after gaining access into the OZ from an outside lane. Like most of the strategies offered thus far, this play incorporates an element of timing due to the positioning of the support forwards. The puck carrier (F1) attempts to pull Xd wide, while his teammates (F2 and F3) interchange. At or around the top of the face-off circle, F1 quickly spins to the outside. If this move is practiced correctly, immediately look to complete a pass to one of the forwards left uncovered by the man-advantage situation produced in front. (See Figure 6.10.)

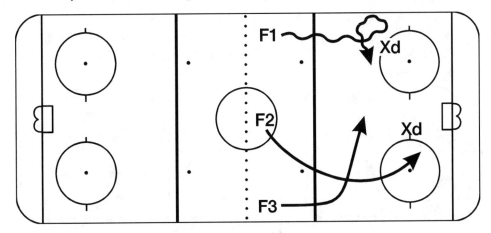

Figure 6.10

D. Should both the puck carrier (F2) and one of the support forwards (F1) find themselves on the same side of the ice, rather than the far Xd, we can attempt to isolate Xd positioned on this side. Note how the "spin-o-rama" here is accompanied by a soft bank pass off the boards. The trailer (F1) now has the momentum to receive the pass left by F2. In turn, F2 has spun towards the boards and is headed towards the slot. Xd is now forced with choosing to pivot and play F1 down low or pick up F2 crashing the net. Such moves, in which players interchange from the corner in an attempt to work a give-&-go towards the opposition's goal, are referred to as "cycling." As with most attempts to overload an area or isolate a man-advantage situation, the path taken by F3 is designed to draw the opposite side Xd wide. (See Figure 6.11.)

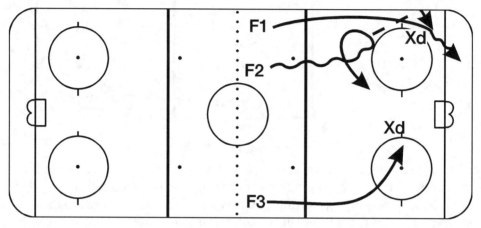

Figure 6.11

E. Similar to those OZ attacks initiated from the middle lane, various seams can be found if our D need to assume an offensive role. In cases where the puck carrier penetrates from an outside lane, defensemen like Paul Coffey and Brian Leetch hit these seams at just the right time and depths. Their timing and positioning rarely force either to forfeit his defensive responsibilities. For example, note the seams created in Figures 6.12 and 6.13. Here, penetration by a D is deep enough to provide offensive support, yet does not overextend beyond the high slot should a defensive role need to be assumed. On those occasions where a D does penetrate deep, at least one of the forwards should always look to offer positional support.

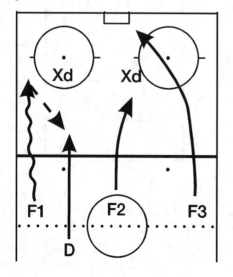

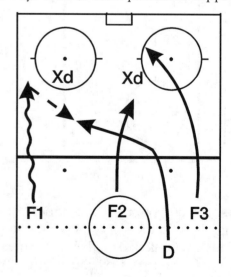

Figure 6.12   **Figure 6.13**

Despite the tactics or strategy designed in our offensive maneuvres, proper positioning dictates that the forward in the high slot serve a defensive purpose as well. Just as earlier chapters mention the importance of a rapid transfer from defense to offense, the same importance exists for its counterpart. Obviously, we are not going to score with every trip into the OZ. More often than not, we may be forced to quickly assume a defensive posture, following a thwarted offensive attempt. Three (or more) men caught deep and/or pinching without support are common errors which cause turnovers and initiate scoring chances against our own goal.

The success of a transition from offense to defense depends on the positioning and play of our own forwards in the OZ. This is most important with the positioning of a man in the high slot. The concept of offensive triangulation allows the same player to exist as scoring threat, while simultaneously placing him in an advantageous position to backcheck or support one of our D pinching/crashing down low. Whether or not we successfully maintain puck control in the OZ, the general positioning assumed by this high forward remains consistent.

Established Puck Control in the Offensive Zone

The previous section of this chapter was dedicated to the progressive offensive flow from NZ to OZ in the form of man-advantage rushes/attacks. They are regarded as highly important, simply because of the opportunity they present upon occurrence. Much literature is devoted to these situations, for it is realized that they represent sound opportunities for scoring. But what of those scoring chances which do not result from the above? Let us begin to examine offensive opportunities created by successful forechecking, puck control, turnovers, etc. In other words, examine plays made to the net not during a rush, but after gaining puck control deep in the OZ.

Although most scoring occurs from within the slot, most scoring opportunities originate from three areas in the OZ. From an offensive (and defensive) standpoint, quickly look to use (or defend) these options upon establishing puck control:

A. Using the Points

Depending on the play and positioning of Xf, look to use our defensemen. If the puck is deep and the opposition's wings are being drawn in below the top of the face-off circles, attempt to feed the open points. Upon this pass being made, both the original puck carrier (F1) and puck-side forward (F2) should already be heading towards the net. This first wave of attack attracts the immediate attention of Xd in front. Meanwhile, the forward positioned off the far post (F3) can slide back to an area attempting to open up a passing lane between himself and the puck-controlling D. Remember that because our forwards have been coached to interchange in the NZ, F3 may represent a wing on his off side. Should the shooting lanes be clogged, a pass to F3 forces the opposition's goaltender to come all the way across the net while picking up the pass through traffic (i.e. one-timer). Should the D elect to shoot, the positioning of our forwards have succeeded in overloading the slot for tip-ins, deflections, and/or rebounds. In this scenario, F3 can slide back into the high slot to assume a defensive responsibility as a forechecker or backchecker, should the shot be blocked or deflected wide. (See Figure 6.14.)

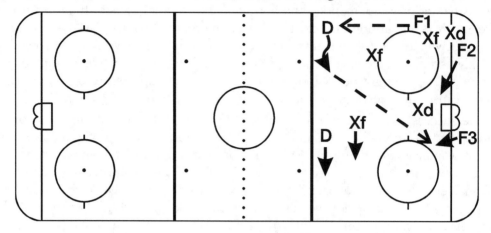

Figure 6.14

In addition to feeding the points up high, examine the option of one D crashing the net. With the puck down low, all eyes are on the puck carrier. Thus, the opposition's wings have their backs turned to their assignments. Simple eye contact with the D may be all that is needed to slip a pass to him penetrating a seam into the slot. Once he has that first step, it will be difficult for Xf to regain positioning between the puck and his assignment. (See Figure 6.15.)

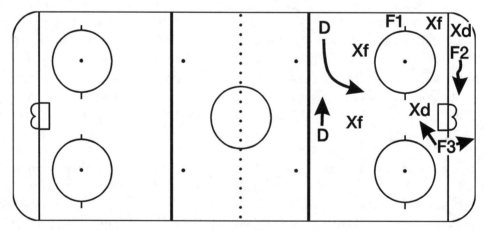

Figure 6.15

B. Working off the Strong Side Boards

If the puck carrier (F1) realizes that the points are being well covered, an alternate option would include setting up a play along the side boards. If the deep man (F2) can spin off of Xd for a moment, a "give-&-go" can be created out of the strong-side corner. (See Figure 6.16a.) Similarly, F1 and F2 can cycle out of the corner attempting to confuse the opposing forward and defenseman covering that side. Should F2 be freed for a moment, F1 can slide a pass to him curling towards the slot area. (See Figure 6.16b.)

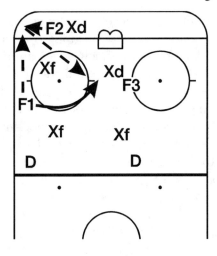

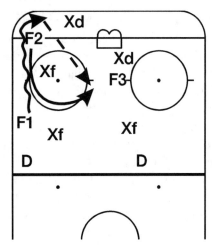

Figure 6.16a   **Figure 6.16b**

C. Reversing the Play

If the puck carrier (F2) finds that either his momentum or the only available lane leads him behind the opposition's net, the support forwards can create one of two different scenarios. Because all eyes will again be on F2, all backs will be facing the blue line. As we have suggested, this gives our D an obvious jump on their coverage. Instructing the support forwards to converge tight on the net causes confusion in front, as well as opening up an outside passing lane for the strong side D to crash. (See Figure 6.17a and 6.17b.) However, we can also instruct the forwards to spread out by setting up wide. This creates more passing lanes in the slot area for circulating through, and/or attacking in waves. Since one Xd must concentrate on the puck carrier, his partner will be forced to pick up the first of our forwards sent to the net. Note how a timed acceleration by the second forward, after the first, can create openings in front. In addition, a wide set up by these forwards also provides an inside passing lane for our D.

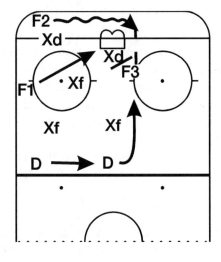

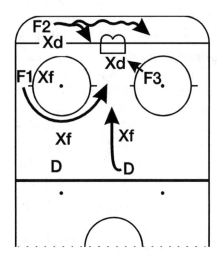

Figure 6.17a   **Figure 6.17b**

Of course originality and improvisation contribute immensely to movement in the OZ. Players who can "read and react" will create many more scoring opportunities than those who wait for the puck. The development of such anticipation is greatly enhanced by familiarity. Whether in the DZ, NZ, or OZ, familiarity breeds confidence, and confidence is a basic principle of success. Teach players fundamentally sound movements, such as the attacking plays detailed above. Similarly, preaching tactics like driving to the net will be rewarded via deflections, rebounds, and/or drawing penalties. Like writing literature and painting on canvas, allow for creativity after players become comfortable with the basic principles of a particular system. Game analyses statements like "they play well together," and "they see the entire ice surface," refer to puck movement without hesitation. It's as if highly skilled players have an innate sense of where their linemates are without requiring visual confirmation. This level of play comes with knowing what to do — and when to do it. Being able to successfully anticipate one's own movements is a prerequisite of knowing what your linemates will most likely do.

How can such spontaneous and impulsive movements, especially like those in the OZ, be anticipated? Both coaching and psychological literature offer three suggestions to the above question:

Repetition - Design drills incorporating basic movements, until they become intuitive and require little "conscious" mental processing. It was mentioned earlier that great hockey players can think one step ahead. Rather than consciously grappling with where to go, players should be examining what to do when they get there. Diagramming, walking through off ice, and progressive design of drills are the first steps of this advanced stage of mental encoding, processing, and retrieval.

Relaxation - If these basic movements are progressively incorporated into practices, they become more familiar to the players. This element of comfort instills a level of confidence and provides answers to formerly time-consuming questions such as, "Where should I be?" or "What is my role?". As players become more comfortable with a system, they become more aware of what is going on around them and, thus, play with increased confidence. Teaching them to recognize systems other teams employ will also instill within them the knowledge and familiarity to counteract with authority and quickness.

Reinforcement - It is hypothesized that continued success and mastery in practice will transfer to games. The positive reinforcement contributed by the coaching staff will add to the acceptance of the system on a group basis. Verbal reinforcement upon successful execution of various movements is continually needed to plant and fertilize the seeds needed for consistency under all scenarios. However, true reinforcement will be manifested by the opportunities gained versus the opposition's tentative movements during a game. At its highest level, reinforcement assumes the many elements of success.

A Return to Positioning in the Offensive Zone

Although all efforts to maintain puck control in the OZ will be exhausted, the positioning of our entire unit must be disciplined. As was mentioned earlier, we do not want to send more than two forwards down low (unless instructed) for fear of getting trapped in deep. Therefore, our forwards must align themselves so as to gain maximum offensive potential, without forfeiting defensive and/or forechecking responsibility.

Game Scenario

Regarding the OZ, where should we be in relation to the puck?

As in the DZ, the weakside wing (F3) must not allow himself to get sucked down low until we have control of the puck. Similar to the off-wing lock system designed by Scotty Bowman, F3 originally positions himself in the high slot at or near the top of the face-off circle. Many coaches refer to this as the "Golden Area" due to the effectiveness achieved by Brett Hull when setting up in this area. With the center and puck-side wing battling deep in the corner, our weak-side wing maintains this high positioning until one of his teammates has the puck. At this point, F3 can drive to the net, or look to set up down low on the opposite side. (See Figures 6.19 and 6.20.) Note that if Xd in front leaves him alone, F3 becomes an open passing option. If Xd is drawn out to F3, a lane to the net may become open for the puckcarrier. Similarly, a passing lane might open and allow our weak-side D to drive to the net. The Colorado Avalanche successfully used this tactic in the 1995-1996 Finals, consistently sending Uwe Krupp and Sandis Ozolinsh to the net.

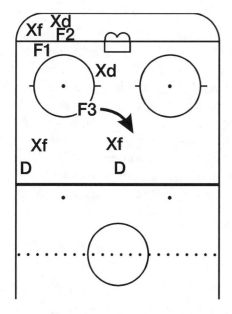

Puck control not yet established
Figure 6.19

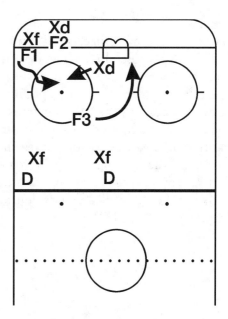

Puck control is established
Figure 6.20

By waiting for the play to develop before breaking to the net, F3 remains in a good defensive position should the opposition gain control of the puck. In addition to becoming an offensive option, his presence can be felt as a forechecker (should the play be reversed), and/or backchecker. The room created, versus being tied up in front with Xd, gives F3 the freedom to assume whichever of these roles is necessary.

Should F2 control the puck behind the net, rather than in the corner, both wings must respond to his movement. Regardless to which side he is flushed, we can still provide immediate and secondary support. For example, if F2 walks out the left side, the puck-side wing drives to the net...taking Xd with him (immediate support). Remind your team that when driving to the net, don't skate by it. Stop in front, cause traffic and anticipate rebounds. If this play can't be made, look for either the weak-side wing or puck-side D crashing the net as a second wave option. (See Figures 6.21 and 6.22.)

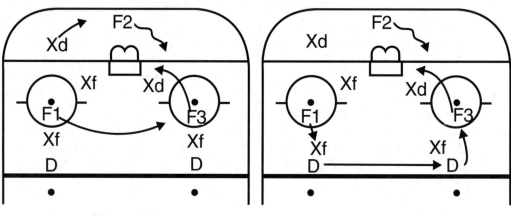

Figure 6.21   **Figure 6.22**

Now that we have successfully gained control of the puck in the OZ, the precise passing and purposeful movement of our forwards have created a scoring opportunity from the slot area. Alas, the puck has been deflected and skids to the far corner. It appears as if a member of the opposition will reach the puck before any of our forwards. Although in the OZ, our transition is now from offense to defense. We have momentarily relinquished puck possession, but because of the positioning of our players, attempts are made to quickly regain control. The quicker we move to pressure the opposition, the less opportunity given for them to assume and exercise breakout options. It is at this point that our transition brings us full circle to where we began our discussion. For a detailed description on forechecking in the OZ, we must return to Chapter 1.

Attacking in the Offensive Zone: A Summary

Man-advantage Rushes

a. From the Middle Lane ...

Triangulation — At some point, one Xd must step up and play the puck carrier as he approaches the slot. This leaves one of the wide support options free.

b. From the Outside Lane ...

Isolation — Either the puck carrier or second forward attempts to draw one Xd out of play by taking him wide or deep. This leaves our third forward to help isolate a 2 on 1 situation versus the remaining Xd.

Established Puck Control in the Offensive Zone

a. Set Up High — Upon gaining puck control, look to use the points if Xf is running around, or getting sucked down below the face-off circles. Once the puck has been played back, forwards can time their attack to the net from various angles and depths.

b. Set Up Low — Moving the puck down low helps buy time for our forwards to circulate towards the net in waves. Similarly, our defensemen can locate open seams from which to penetrate.

— Whether set up high or down low, have at least one player momentarily fade behind the view of the opposition. Because most eyes will be on the puck (in the corner, behind the net, at the point), the element of surprise created by this movement often creates scoring opportunities.

Where should I be in relation to the puck?

Until we have puck possession, the weak-side wing remains in the high slot. Should puck control be gained, drive to the net, or set up down low on the opposite side. Should puck control be lost, look to forecheck (if reversed) or backcheck through the far lane.

Teaching Offensive Team Play

Preach creativity, after mastery of basic positioning and movements. This mastery is achieved through:

Repetition — constant diagramming, drills, and teaching.

Relaxation — with knowledge comes familiarity and confidence.

Reinforcement — success manifested via transfer from practice to game situa
tions.

Similar to its counterpart, the continuous movement required by offensive team play should be taught from a progressive approach. The mastery of basic attack formations serves to enhance the creativity needed to develop man-advantage situations. Within this development matures the skating, passing, and shooting skills required for success in the Offensive Zone. The execution of such movements are based on elements including frequency, timing, and accuracy — all of which must be incorporated into practices. This level of maturation is greatly influenced by the ability of a coaching staff to further design progressive drills prompting creativity and originality under game conditions. Thus, the implementation of such drills should follow this pattern:

Step 1. Familiarity and Instinct

Design unit movements with no oppositional resistance. Include transitional elements from defense to offense, and allow for creativity after success with basic maneuvres.

Step 2. Creation of Man-Advantage Situations

Employ drills in all 3 zones against a smaller number of opposition. Players will begin to isolate and move in ways creating man-advantage situations.

Step 3. Read and React

Design offensive movements within each zone against organized defensive schemes. Have the opposing units first play with their sticks reversed. After seeing successfully coordinated movements by the offense, allow the opposition to use their sticks as normal.

Step 4. Movement with a Purpose

Offensive team movements are initiated from the Defensive and Neutral Zones, with the goal of penetrating the Offensive Zone and creating a scoring opportunity.

Step 5. Simulate Game Conditions

Plan a controlled scrimmage aimed at offensive team play in all three zones. Have players be prepared to stop on the whistle in order to correct positional problems.

SECTION III
Special Teams Play

T he conclusion of the regular season brings with it a feeling of latent apprehension. Upon the horizon now lies a level of play driven by sheer heart and determination. For those who have not experienced its magic, post season ice hockey is equated with the consummate sacrifice of mind and body — for the sake of team and teammates. For those who have walked in its path, the post season offers an opportunity to fulfill one's dreams.

In one game, which I will never forget, I had a particularly memorable view as a spectator, not a player. Although I did not start in goal that night, I was just as excited about going to the playoffs as everyone else. I would have given anything to be in there, for the "hero" versus "goat" debate does not exist within my personality. I'd take such a risk any day. During the morning pregame skate, coach mentioned to us that a few scouts would be in attendance that evening. Combining post season play with the opportunity to prove oneself in front of a major league scout constitutes the recipe for a great calibre of hockey.

Many talented young hockey players existed on our team. However, there was a veteran defenseman who had brought his game to new levels over the last month of the regular season. He had begun to receive much press exposure as a result of his play. In fact, the "spurts" and "glimpses" of talent seen needed a challenge of this magnitude to fuse. To say that he "came to play" that evening would be an understatement, for after two periods he remained a plus three with three assists. Early in the third period he dropped to block a shot, which was absorbed in the midsection. Sitting down at one end of the bench, I helped him over the boards as play continued. It was obvious that he was in severe pain. Our trainer scrambled down to assist. Evaluating the physical and verbal responses while pushing, probing, and feeling, the trainer determined that the puck may have broken "at least" one rib. Although the player continued to deny the pain, it was clearly evident. A subtle yet heated argument between the two ensued as to whether or not he could continue. Our coach yelled down to the trainer for a diagnosis and recommendation, but his attention was suddenly directed to something that had occurred on the ice. At that moment the defenseman pulled the trainer, now standing in front of him, face to face. With words and a facial expression I will never forget, he pleaded, "This may be the only chance I'll ever get." Eye contact between the two was again interrupted by our coach. "Well, can he go?" After looking at both of us, the trainer requested a few minutes to help strap on a flack jacket to what he diagnosed as "bruised ribs." He missed only one shift and played the entire third period with a fractured rib.

The heart and determination depicted here are representative of most pregame locker room stories. Before stepping on the ice, I often remind my players of all the blocked shots, weekends sacrificed while growing up, and hours logged on the road en route to another game. Each outing provides the opportunity for improvement and possibly recognition. Successful application and transferral of such a philosophy is targeted at all areas of play. Whether with the puck or away from the puck, players mature as they appreciate and accept various roles. These roles may be emphasized in man-advantage, man-disadvantage, and face-off situations. Under such circumstances, qualities and sacrifice such as those in the above account are often called upon. Here, the scenarios are presented as "Special Teams Play." Note the word "team" in this title. Make sure players recognize both its value and meaning. Remember, coaches lead by example. The attitude with which you approach each facet of the game is contagious ... and will be caught by your players.

7

The Powerplay

"We are told that talent creates its own opportunities. But it is sometimes that intense desire creates not only its opportunities, but its own talents." — Eric Hoffer, The Passionate State of Mind

It is very possible that consistent execution of all things described thus far will result in a different form of "man-advantage" situation. Hard work, effective anticipation, and rapid transitions can actually manipulate our opponents out of position. In some instances, they may be forced to take penalties in an attempt to nullify that the proximal advantages gained do not surrender scoring chances ... if not out of frustration itself. These man-advantage situations offer substantial and favorable circumstances for offensive opportunities.

In order for these circumstances to prove favorable, the powerplay must be executed correctly. Keep in mind, that its effectiveness is contingent upon the conjugation of four interacting factors:

1. Passing
2. Penetration
3. Positioning
4. Patience

Although each focuses on a separate entity, like the 5-man unit on the ice, success requires that each be represented. In addition, representation must exist within all three zones of play. Because the first task involves successful movement out of the DZ, let us begin our discussion assuming that we have gained puck control following a dump in.

Breaking Out of the Defensive Zone

In most penalty kill situations, it is common practice to employ modified versions of a "1-man" or "Trap" forechecking scheme. The positioning and intent are modified to compensate for the man-disadvantage. The role assumed by the first forechecker may follow the "logo" guideline presented in earlier chapters, depending on whether puck control has yet been established. Within the context of a powerplay, the element of passing typically results in immediate conscious retrieval of that which causes the opposition's "box" (or diamond) to collapse. Yes, passing in the OZ is critical to the success of any powerplay. However, such "visions of grandeur" are preconditioned back in the DZ following a successful breakout.

Ideally, it is our goal to spread the opposition out and create the space needed to enhance puck movement beyond the DZ. It is not uncommon to see forwards set up well within the NZ during a powerplay breakout. Such tactics are designed to pull Xd off the blue line. This is referred to as "stretching" the defense. Although creating a man-advantage situation down low, it is the movement of the entire unit which determines success. As we have already learned, completion of the first pass is again critical. (See Figure 7.1.)

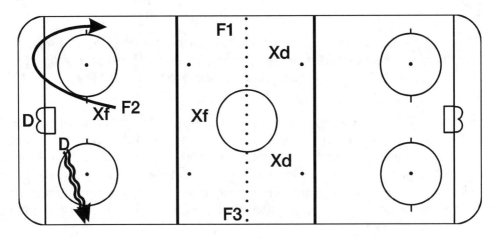

Figure 7.1

A. D1, realizing that he is not being chased, has several options once puck control is established. Should the deep forechecker lock on to the movement of our first forward (F2) curling to the outside, D1 can carry the puck up the opposite side. His partner, D2, assumes a wide but not yet parallel position off the far post. The support forwards (F1 & F3), originally set up in the NZ, accelerate off the boards filling the vacant lanes in unison with F2. Notice how the puck-side forward (F3) stretches Xd by taking him deep, before cutting to the middle. (See Figure 7.2.)

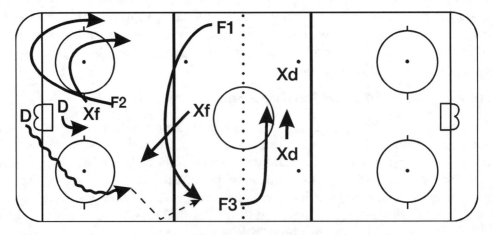

Figure 7.2

At the point of confrontation with the forecheckers, D1 has the option of headmanning to one of these forwards, dumping the puck into the OZ (if given access to the red line) or reversing the flow by passing to his partner. The three options are outlined below. In the first two of these scenarios, remember that we have F2 accelerating along the outside lane should we attempt to employ the D & A principle. (See Figure 7.3.)

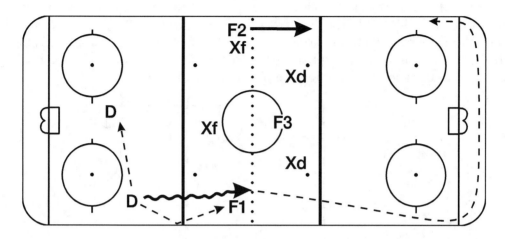

Figure 7.3

B.1 Rather than locking on to a particular assignment, the deep forechecker may set up in front of the net and attempt to manipulate the movement of D1. In this situation, D2 can go immediately to the hash marks on his respective side. Similarly, the first forward back (F2) swings "low" out of the opposite corner. A simple reverse by D1 may be all that is needed to draw the forechecker one way, thus opening up the far side. Design paths taken by the support forwards (F1 & F3) to complement this first pass, with at least two passing options available to the puck carrier. Again, a deep path taken by the puck-side forward opens up the blue line by stretching Xd into the NZ. (See Figure 7.4.)

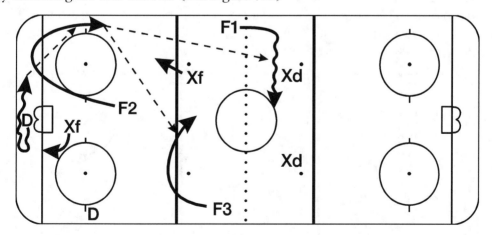

Figure 7.4

Once the NZ is accessed, look to headman or dump to an "accelerating" team-mate. Depending on the aggressiveness of the penalty kill unit, we may be permitted to carry the puck into the OZ. Regardless of how gained, it is our goal to "control the play" within all three zones when faced with a powerplay situation.

B.2 An adaptation to breaking out, when the deep forechecker sets up in front, involves the first forward back (F2) swinging behind the net to pick up the puck from D1. As F2 draws the forechecker to one side, the puck is played: a) back to D1; or, b) across to D2. The forwards positioned in the NZ (F1 & F3) move in support of this pass. F3 (on the opposite side) comes across on his forehand, while F1 (puck side) heads deep and across, stretching Xd. F2 continues his path along the far outside lane, unless otherwise directed. (See Figure 7.5.)

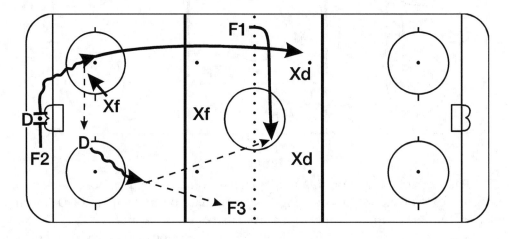

Figure 7.5

C. Should D1 feel immediate pressure from one to two forecheckers, look to use D2 behind the net or in the far corner in an attempt to reverse the flow. The first forward back (F2) must read the play and hustle back puck-side. The forward normally setting up in the NZ on that side (F3) can easily slide down along the boards into the DZ. Because F3 has slid down to this area, Xd will most likely position himself on the point. If this occurs, look for F2 occupying a wide open middle lane. (See Figure 7.6.)

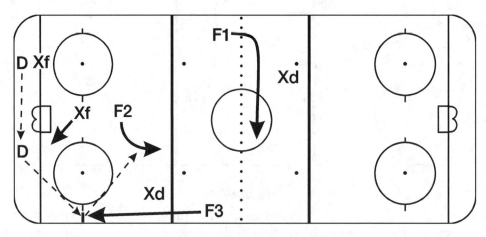

Figure 7.6

Once in the NZ, coaches are invited to review the section on opposite corner dumps and/ or wraps in an effort to "aid" in their design of penetrating the OZ. In order to exploit the man-advantage in this scenario, it may prove necessary to send two forwards down deep. Here, the man-advantage situation (represented as a 2 on 1) increases the probability of regaining puck control. Any creative modifications in the design of player movement through both the NZ and OZ, which sustain this advantage, are encouraged.

If presented, alternate routes of OZ penetration involve constant control (i.e. carrying/passing the puck). Should the puck carrier have or recognize a passing option within an open lane to the OZ, there must exist a designated area from which to set up the powerplay. Whether along the point, halfway along the boards, or down low, our final destination will include movement towards the net. This is created by proper positioning.

At this point let us resume our discussion following successful penetration of the OZ — with puck control. Note that the systems presented here can be utilized in both a 5 on 4 and 5 on 3 situation.

The Overload

Regardless of where a coach wants to set up the powerplay, the subsequent movement of all those on the ice must support the original positioning of the puck carrier. For example, control along the boards provides the "additional" options of setting up down low, versus up high. Both arise from the tactical application of situating three players on one side of the ice. This set-up is designed to exploit one half of the opposition's box by creating a man-advantage or 3 on 2 situation. From this position, we can initiate movement to the net with: a) a pass to the forward (F1) down in the corner; or, b) a pass to D1 at the point. The option chosen may depend on where the opposing forward (Xf) on that side of the box is located.

A. If Xf is complacent, or attempts to negate the high option by closing those passing lanes to the points, we may be able to work a "give-&-go" and/or "cycle" out of the corner. Note how F2 and F1 have isolated a 2 on 1 situation down low in both scenarios. With the opposition's forwards covering the points and one Xd forced to cover F3 in front, coordinated movement by the two puck-side forwards should create an offensive opportunity. (See Figures 7.7 and 7.8.)

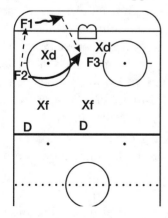

Figure 7.7

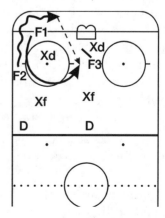

Figure 7.8

B. Further modifications of this low option may include the puck-controlling forward (F2) sliding down to the corner. Rather than cycling up those same boards, the low support forward (F1) simultaneously slides behind the far post to receive a pass. This movement creates a man-advantage situation around the net. Here, F1 forces Xd in front to make a split-second decision. If Xd stays with F3 in front, F1 can attempt to walk the puck out. If Xd plays F1, then F3 is left alone. In addition, now that all attention is focused on this area (and averted from the rest of the zone), it is encouraged to design movements sending both F2 and/or D2 to the net. Such paths taken are referred to as "back door" plays and can prove quite effective because of their abruptness. (See Figures 7.9 and 7.10.)

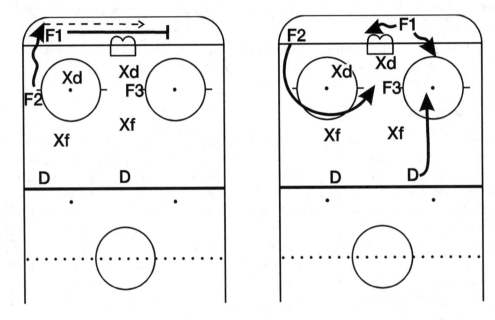

Figure 7.9   Figure 7.10

The Umbrella

Suppose we notice that the opposing wings are getting sucked below the top of the face-off circles? Such undisciplined movements prompt us to begin looking to use our points. A widely practiced play initiated by feeding the puck up high is referred to as the "D-Slide." A defenseman (D1), whom has been selected to quarterback the powerplay, slides to the middle after receiving a pass from F2. His partner (D2) drops to an area between the blue line and opposite face-off circle, while F2 slides out to the same area on his side. F3 maintains his position in the high slot, whereas F1 can set up low off either post. (Figure 7.11.)

Note how the co-ordinated slide results in a shift from an "Overload" to "Umbrella" alignment. The puck-controlling D must assess the best of several immediate options:

A. An aggressive approach by the high Xf on that side opens up a return pass to F2 positioned off the boards. Here, we have created another man-advantage situation with F1 coming out of the corner. In addition, look to have D2 slice the middle of the box formation from his position off the opposite side face-off circle. Remember, all eyes will be on movement of the puck and not on D2 who has drifted momentarily out of view. (See Figure 7.12.)

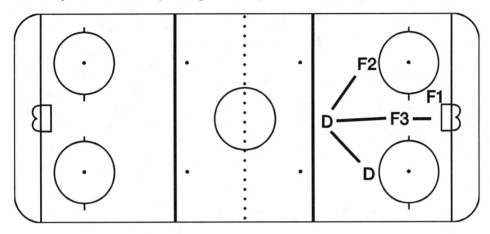

Figure 7.11

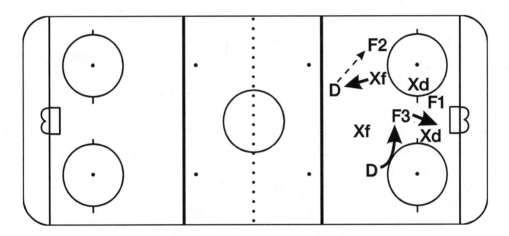

Figure 7.12

B. Should the opposite high Xf attack the middle, look for D2 who has maneuvred into an unprotected area. The support forwards, having identified this option, penetrate the slot accordingly. Similar to the unannounced path taken by D2 above, F2 can crash from his position off the top of the face-off circle. F1 converges by taking a path either in front of, or behind the net (depending on which post he is to set up). F3 continues to tie up, as well as distract, both the goalie and Xd in front. Keeping both hands on the stick allows F to "plant" himself in front by increasing his balance. (See Figure 7.13.)

C. Should neither Xf pressure D1, our quarterback also has the option of shooting the puck. The support forwards, already moving towards the net, will be in position for deflections and/or rebounds. Note how the area assumed by F3 lies directly between the puck and the goal. His duties include deflections, screening the goaltender, and fighting off checks should a rebound exist. Similarly, the path taken to the net by F1 sets him just off the post. His timed acceleration from the

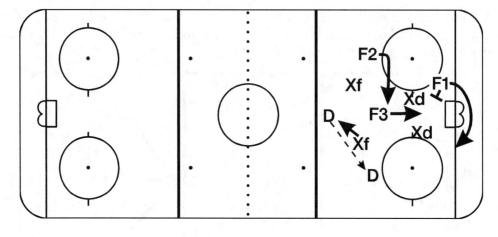

Figure 7.13

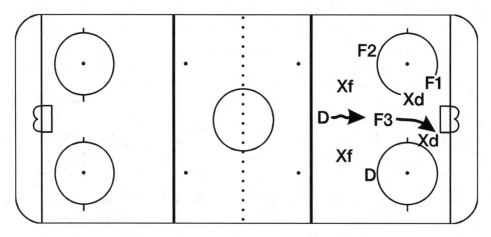

Figure 7.14

corner increases the likelihood of a tip-in opportunity or rebound conversion. (See Figure 7.14.)

Pick Plays

Today's version of ice hockey, especially regarding the powerplay, possesses features similar to other sports. Through the course of semantic evolution, hockey now shares such terms as "quarterback" and "special teams." Designed movements incorporating "picks" and "screens" are being increasingly employed. Similar to a "three-step drop" used in football, the stationary positioning from which a powerplay begins permits commencement from say, the third pass. Even if between the same two players, this third pass may initiate designed movement of the entire unit. Therefore, all must know their roles and remain patient in awaiting to fulfill them. One, two, three ... Surprise! By the time the third pass is completed, the powerplay unit has strategically maneuvred into a better scoring position. These movements may (or may not) include players off the puck to provide picks and/or screens in attempts for those designated to get open more easily.

A. For example, the third pass between D1 and F2 is allowed through to F1 waiting in the corner. The screen provided causes the brief moment of hesitation needed to suddenly spring F2 off the boards and towards the slot. (See Figure 7.15.)

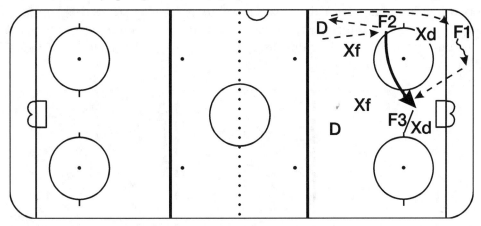

Figure 7.15

Note how the return pass from F2, back to D1, forces Xf on that side to remain close to the point. Thus, playing the following pass out of the corner creates a man-advantage situation down low.

B. A modified version of this play has F2 setting a pick for F1. Again, our use of D1 keeps Xf on that side close to the point. Once the third pass leaves the stick of D1, F1 is already accelerating up the boards. F2, knowing his role, simultaneously leaves the boards and attempts to gain an inside position on Xd in front. By the time of completion, F1 is curling full speed towards the slot with the puck. Should the opposite Xd play the puck carrier, F3 (already in front) can slide to the far post. (See Figure 7.16.)

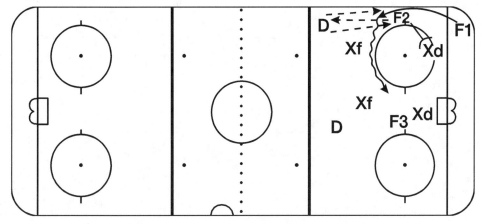

Figure 7.16

C. A similar play has F2 setting a pick for D2. The third pass is again allowed through to F1 in the corner. In the meantime, F2 has left the boards on his way to the net. Once receiving the puck, F1 passes to F3 who has slid down behind the far post. F2 will be granted outside positioning in front, simply because Xd will wish to remain between the puck and net. Rather than fight this coverage, use it to the fullest advantage. By allowing Xd to position himself between F2 and F3, we have trapped him in tight. A back door path taken to the net by D2, places him in good scoring position with a teammate off each post. All the attention will be focused on F2 crashing from the side boards, although the primary play is designed to hit D2 crashing from up top. (See Figure 7.17.)

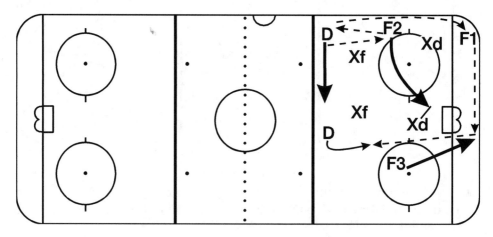

Figure 7.17

Emphasizing patience allows us to use the very effective element of "surprise." Disciplined movements greatly deter the opposition's ability to anticipate what we will do. The plays detailed above are mere examples of the flexibility and original-ity which exist in design. Their inclusion, it is hoped, will serve to further whet the creative appetites of those coaches who enjoy this element of the game.

The Powerplay: A Summary

Successful execution is contingent upon four interacting factors, in all three zones.

1. Passing
2. Penetration
3. Positioning
4. Patience

When designing powerplay breakouts, attempt to spread the opposition out to create open passing and skating lanes. It may prove necessary to stretch Xd by sending at least one forward into the NZ. This opens up the blue line on that side.

In the Offensive Zone...

The Overload — By positioning three men on one side of the ice, we numerically gain a man-advantage. From this position, we can initiate simultaneous movement to the net from both the strong and weak sides.

The Umbrella — Rather than overloading one side of the ice, this formation creates a man-advantage at different depths in the Offensive Zone. Similar to the triangulation concept introduced with odd-man rushes, the puck carrier (occupying the middle lane) forces the high forward covering him to commit, leaving the support option on that side open.

Pick Plays — Designed movements requiring a player to pick/screen the opposition, enabling the puck carrier easier access to the net. Often these plays are initiated from a specific number of passes.

With two or more F's battling down low and we are forced to use the points, our D can buy time by moving the puck to the middle. This creates more options and gives the forwards time to re-establish their positioning and/or get to the net.

8

Penalty Killing

"If it is said that individual character is manifested via one's actions, then team character must be comprised of a comprehensive response to various conditions. Should team character be founded upon idealistic principles including discipline, unity, determination, and the like ... team response will be most productive." — Anonymous

In summation of the above quote, it is the combined mental and physical efforts of the entire unit which promotes success. Much of the offensive systems detailed in this book, focus on creating a man-advantage situation as a definite enhancement to scoring potential. Penalty killing, because this very situation is already provided, grants the opposition an obvious advantage should we not be prepared.

For a discussion on defending "against" a powerplay, let us assume that our penalty killing unit has successfully cleared the puck the length of the ice. The opposing Xd have set up in their own zone and are awaiting Xf to assume their breakout positions.

In the Offensive Zone

A. In the OZ, the most prominent forechecking system assumes the formation of an upside down letter "Y." Here, F1 positions himself off one post in an attempt to flush the puck carrier (Xd) one way. F2, located in the high slot, can now get a jump on the first pass without telegraphing in that direction. Both D are responsible for closing any passing lanes into the NZ. (See Figure 8.1.)

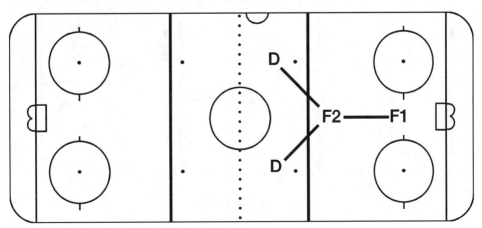

Figure 8.1

B. Should either Xd or an opposing forward attempt to walk out from behind the net, F1 can flush this puck carrier wide by taking an inside angle. F2 negates any cross-ice options by clogging the middle lanes. This positioning means that passes intended for players located on the far side must first pass through F2. (See Figure 8.2.)

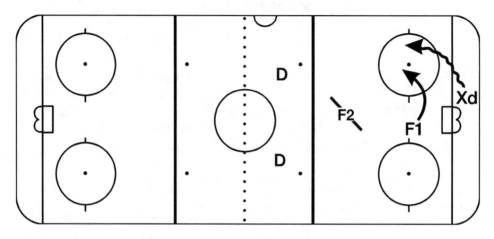

Figure 8.2

C. If the option of regrouping or changing the point of attack is exercised, a disciplined rotation between both of our forwards may be required. In this example, Xd walks the puck out and is flushed wide by F1. Xd slides the puck across to his partner who attempts to continue the breakout from the opposite side. F2, facing the play, steps up and flushes the new puck carrier wide. The momentum achieved by F1 takes him right back to the middle lanes vacated by F2. The coordinated rotation by these two penalty-killing forwards, because it involves circular paths re-emerging in the middle lane, is commonly referred to as "circulating." (See Figure 8.3.)

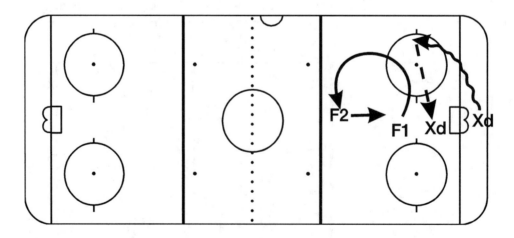

Figure 8.3

In the Neutral Zone

Should the opposition be successful in gaining access into the NZ, coverage remains consistent with that emphasized in earlier sections on backchecking. However, the first forward back (F1) must extend his outside lane coverage. Rather than locking on to the wide wing (Xf), F1 comes back in line with the far post. By assuming this path, three tactical obligations are fulfilled:

1. The positioning of F1 remains between the puck and wide wing. This negates using Xf as a headman outlet.

2. Because the puck carrier will not want to play into the backchecking forward, F1 indirectly flushes him to one side of the ice. Not only does this make it easier for our D to play, but also insures sufficient coverage (two men) should the puck be played into the far corner.

3. The path assumed by F1 is consistent with that line taken should the opposition establish puck control in our zone (i.e., off the far post). Therefore, running around in an attempt to set up our DZ coverage will be minimized. (See Figure 8.4.)

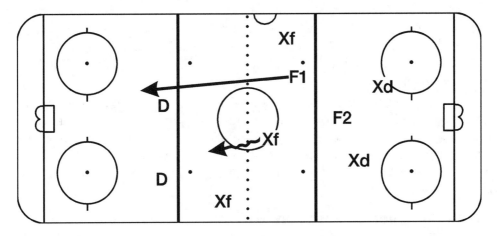

Figure 8.4

The deep forward (F2) should be instructed to come back through the middle for the same reasons ascribed in Chapter 2. These include:

1. To prevent the option of regrouping.

2. To be in position to pick up Xd jumping into the rush.

3. To serve as a rapid transition outlet should a turnover occur.

Yet, the path taken should be in line with the opposition's puck movement. For example, if they attempt to set up on the left side, F2 takes a path "from the middle out to that side." (See Figure 8.5.)

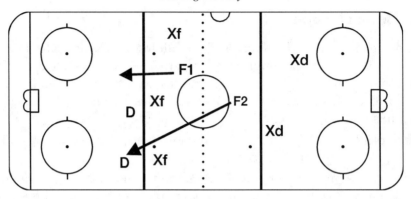

Figure 8.5

In the Defensive Zone

For many programs, penalty killing in the DZ is limited to a "box" formation. History has dictated that disciplined execution can prove quite successful. Indeed, a majority of coaches at all levels adhere to this approach. However, as we shall see, it may prove advantageous to install alternate systems. After all, without the luxury of scouting reports, we design most powerplays against a box formation. So, why not play the odds that our coaching counterparts are doing the same? Serving the unexpected will add to the hesitation, confusion, and frustration of most opposition movements.

It is at this point that we will begin to examine the most productive penalty kill formations, versus various powerplay set-ups. Keep in mind, the intent here is to simply add to a coach's arsenal and educate players. Familiarity with these options better prepares us for many, perhaps all, situations we will face. For discussion purposes, let us assume that the opposition's powerplay unit has established puck control in our zone.

Versus the Overload (set up low)

The Overload involves an attempt to outnumber, or gain a man advantage, within a certain area of ice. In a powerplay situation, the opposition may spread three men out along the OZ boards and two in front of our net. Because we must cover the latter, a man advantage exists along the outside lane. One of our goals is to keep it there. Thus, the formation of a "tight box" offers the best solution for limiting puck movement to the perimeter. Stops and starts, rather than curling away from the puck carrier, negates the chance that access into the slot will be gained by the opposition faking a pass or shot. A constant reminder to keep sticks on the ice makes it more difficult for those on the powerplay to complete passes targeted for the weak side. Full use of one's peripheral vision enables players to focus beyond the puck. The more ice visualized, the less opportunity for an unsuspecting player to crash or slice without being noticed. Finally, communication between all five players is crucial. Remember, the fifth player is represented as the goaltender who probably possesses the best view of anyone out there. With the puck being moved around the perimeter, not posing an immediate scoring threat, the goaltender can quickly glance away to see if any weak-side players are maneuvering into open areas. He can then inform the defensive unit, either verbally and/or by banging his stick, as to what is going on beyond their view. Reinforce the goaltender's efforts to serve as quarterback for the penalty-killing unit. (See Figure 8.6.)

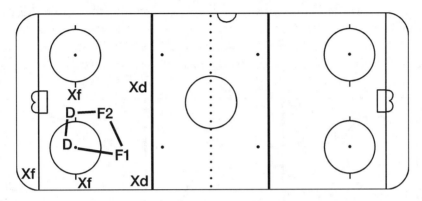

Figure 8.6

Once the box has been set up, it's important to skate in straight lines between various points. These points are represented as the recipients of opposition passes. Although a player may believe that his momentum will be more easily transferred in the opposite direction by curling one way, he must be disciplined and stop with puck movement. For example, an overload situation involves an exchange of passes between the two low opposing forwards. Our D on that side cannot allow himself to spin away from either Xf. By doing so, he momentarily turns his back to both the puck and player he is skating away from. (See Figure 8.7a.) A good hockey team will be able to take advantage of such undisciplined movements and spring one of these two forwards. Similarly, spinning towards either forward reverses the momentum needed to pick up Xf crashing the net. Our D will find it very difficult after curling to the outside to cover a player breaking to the inside. (See Figure 8.7b.)

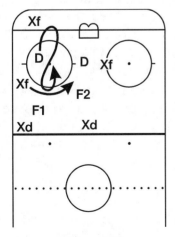

Figure 8.7a

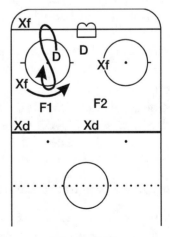

Figure 8.7b

Coaches should demonstrate "why" some movements are more tactically correct than others. Teach the penalty-killing unit to use stops and starts, and allow them to see how the momentum shifts caused by spinning off a man can take one out of position.

If the play is worked down low, the forward covering the weak side (F2), can slide into the high slot to offer support. However, should the weak-side Xd crash, he remains the responsibility of F2. The forward covering the strong-side point (F1) can take a step towards the middle to deter any cross-ice passes. (See Figure 8.8.)

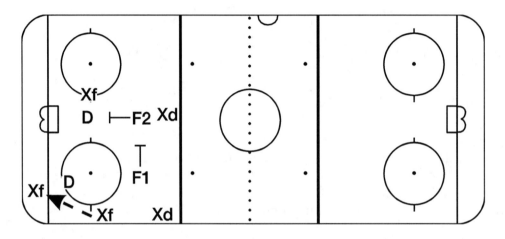

Figure 8.8

Most problems arise when one of the penalty killers gets sucked out of position. Allow the opposition to move the puck outside the box. Let them take the long and/or poor angle shots. Not only are these easier for the goaltender to handle, an inaccurate shot often serves as a turnover. Don't forget, the momentum of Xf is incoming. A wide shot may prove easier for our players to retrieve because they do not have to reverse their momentum, as do Xf crashing the net.

As noted, the movement of F2 serves as defensive support in the high slot area. Similarly, both D must move in support of each other. Neither D should extend himself into the perimeter unless a free puck exists. Nor should they follow the puck carrier behind the net, but instead relinquish coverage to a partner. Beware of the opposition crashing down low. The guideline for teaching this is as follows:

Once the puck carrier has passed behind the net into D2's half of the ice and he yells "Mine!," D1 spins to the inside while looking to pick up anyone penetrating within the box. Warn players not to become mesmerized by the puck. Regardless of the level of discipline, one of the two high forwards may still need to lock on to an opposing player sent to the net.

Versus the Overload (set up high)

True, the formation of a box can be adjusted by coaching staffs to successfully defend against any overload situation. Even if the puck is played back to the points, the penalty-killing unit simply adheres to the principles described earlier. The main difference lies with the movement of the opposition's powerplay. More often than not, Xd will walk the puck towards the middle. Against a box formation, this movement is successful in creating a man-advantage situation in the area from which the puck is being moved away from. How? If undisciplined, both of our high forwards are drawn laterally with Xd. Note how F2 especially can be taken out of the play due to the movement imposed by F1. (See Figure 8.9.)

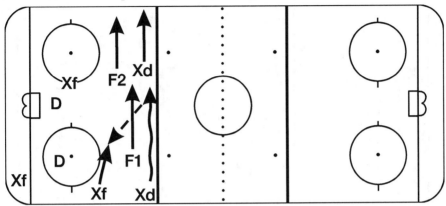

Figure 8.9

A more productive system involves a rotation between these two high forwards. Once Xd has committed towards the middle, allow F1 to relinquish coverage to F2. F1, in turn, slides back to an area negating a return pass to the strong side. This forces the opposition to change their attack. D1 no longer has to worry about a 2 on 1 situation and can attend to the area in front of the net. The weak side D2, originally positioned off the far post, can now slide out in anticipation of Xd passing to his partner at the top of the face-off circle. Here, our box has transformed into a "diamond" formation. Combining two previously distinct approaches has proven quite successful and is being increasingly adopted in most professional systems. The attempt to create any type of man-advantage situation in front is defended by sliding that player positioned on the weak side down low to offer defensive support. In the example below, note the lateral freedom given to F1 in reading and defending the option exercised by Xd. (See Figure 8.10.)

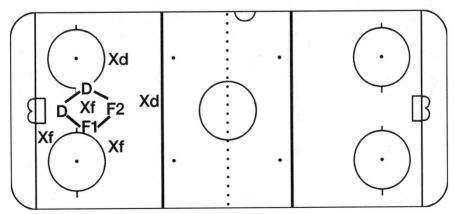

Figure 8.10

Versus the Umbrella

Although the above oppositional movements subsequently create an "Umbrella," they actually represent a forced result by our penalty-killing unit. Should we recognize immediate attempts to set up, rather than converting to this formation, proper positioning can assume the shape of an upside down "T." (See Figure 8.11.)

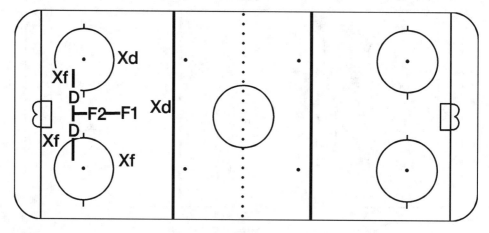

Figure 8.11

There obviously is little need to cover one high man with two forwards. The positioning of F2 behind F1 helps to define certain responsibilities. Whichever direction Xd attempts to move the puck (left or right), F2 reacts by pressuring that recipient. F1 slides down to deter any cross-ice options, as well as negate any return passes to the original puck carrier. Any rotations by these forwards, following the puck being successfully played back to Xd, remain the decision of the coaching staff. It is the duty of both D to box out those Xf attempting to gain position in front of our net. (See Figure 8.12.)

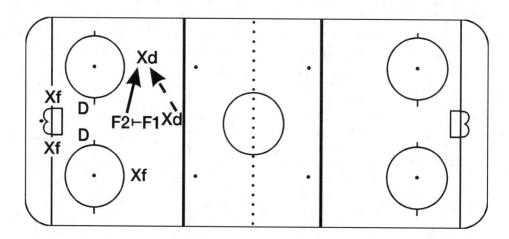

Figure 8.12

Penalty Killing: A Summary

In the Offensive Zone ...

The most prominent forechecking schemes are conservative in design. Unless the situation dictates otherwise, F1 sets up in the high slot. This insures that the first forechecker doesn't get caught deep in the Offensive Zone.

In the Neutral Zone ...

The paths taken by the backchecking forwards remain consistent.

The puck-side F can stand up at red line if supported. By forcing X to headman the puck, miscues can result as incomplete passes and/or icings.

In the Defensive zone ...

Versus the Overload — Depending on whether set up low or high, variations of a "box" formation have proven most successful.

Versus the Umbrella — Should the "Overload" be walked into an "Umbrella," our box can transform into a diamond formation.

— If immediate attempts are designed to set up the "Umbrella," strategic placement of F2 behind F1 enables immediate pressure following the first pass.

When killing penalties, keep sticks in the ice or to the middle. Limit puck movement to the perimeter and negate penetration to the middle.

Scouting reports should help us key on X's primary playmaker. When this player has the puck, pressure him and don't give him time to set up.

9

Face-Offs

Consistent with the flow of play depicted in Section II of this book, we will here examine face-offs as they occur in the:

a. Defensive Zone

b. Neutral Zone

c. Offensive Zone

Note that although player movement following a face-off is dependent on whether the draw is won or lost, it is also dependent on whether the preconceived play is to "push" the puck ahead or "pull" it back. In each case, the forwards must already know what roles and lanes they are responsible for in light of puck possession. Remember, every face-off represents an opportunity to gain or surrender puck control.

Defensive Zone Face-Offs

One might immediately conclude that the primary objective with DZ draws includes pulling the puck back to one of our defensemen in an attempt to regroup and break out. True, most DZ scenarios define success via this execution.

A. For example, should the opposition line up in a standard formation, with a wing on each hash mark, reversing behind the net to open ice represents the most logical option. After all, a reverse requires the entire opposing unit to shift across the ice. (Figure 9.1.)

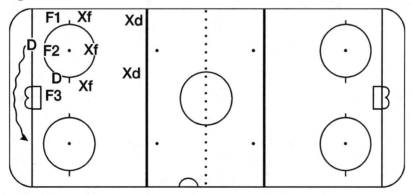

Figure 9.1

103

Whether F2 is successful in winning the draw, or F1 has to come in and tap back to D1, F3 is already accelerating to the opposite side boards. Note the role of D2 is to screen the only opposing forward with immediate access to this side of the ice. The passing outlet for F3 could be created by either of the two remaining forwards. Should F2 win the draw cleanly, he can spin off his check and angle towards this far point. The ease of this maneuvre will be enhanced if the opposing center is directed to forecheck D1. (See Figure 9.2.)

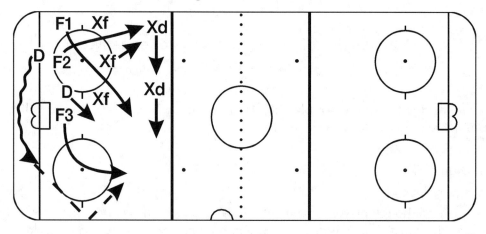

Figure 9.2

If the draw is not won and F2 is forced to tie up his man, quick movement to the middle by F1 enables him to tap the puck back to D1. His continued momentum will offer a lane leading to open ice and provide a passing outlet for D1. Again, D2 is responsible for screening out the opposing wing on this side of the ice. (See Figure 9.3.)

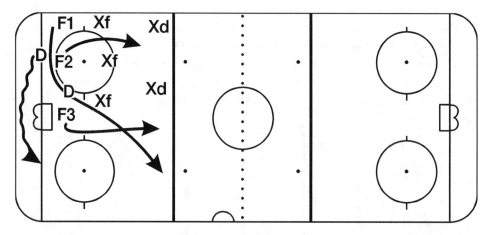

Figure 9.3

Whichever scenario occurs, the forward remaining on the original side of the ice can attempt to "separate" the opposition's defense by moving into the NZ. Not only does this take Xd wide and off the blue line, but it helps to create a man-advantage situation on the far side. Positioning D2 parallel with the three forwards gives us an extra man at puck level. Take this into account when defining responsibilities after both gaining or surrendering puck control.

Common variations in face-off positioning include shifting the board-side wing behind the center or placing both wings along the inside hash mark. In both cases, the board-side wing (F1) is left alone. In addition to pulling the draw back, F2 now has another option. Should his forehand lead to the boards, he may be instructed to push the puck to this open wing. Centers such as Craig MacTavish and Neal Broten are remarkable in adjusting the positioning of their body to complement this effort. Rather than lining up square to the face-off dot, they position their feet to one side. This allows them to twist their body for more power, as well as gain inside or outside positioning. Remember, the visiting centerman has to put his stick down first. Learn to read his body language, the grip on his stick and the alignment of his teammates.

If we examine these two face-off alignments more closely, it becomes clear as to what our preferred counterattack might be:

B. For example, if the opposing wing lines up at the top of the face-off circle, F2 should attempt to draw the puck back to D1. Note how a quick reverse simulates the play diagrammed earlier. D2 screens his assignment, and F3 breaks for the far boards. If in need of a goal, look to sneak an uncovered F1 behind Xd during the reverse movement. Xd may get mesmerized by the puck, or distracted, and momentarily forget about this wing. After initially remaining stationary, a sudden accelerated path across the NZ may open a passing lane beyond or between Xd. Long passes such as these are difficult to make and need to be practiced. (See Figure 9.4.)

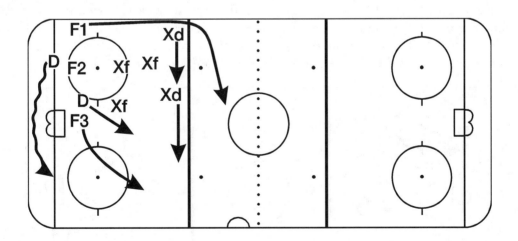

Figure 9.4

C. However, if both opposing wings set up along the inside hash mark, this far lane no longer exists. We now return to the option of using F1 along the boards. Apart from attempting to reverse the play or sliding the puck into the NZ, are there any ways to headman with possession? Yes, but each requires the puck to beat at least one oncoming player.

If the draw is played directly outward from F2 to F1, look for D2 to screen inside while F3 spins off his check as a passing option. The key to this, like most face-offs, is getting a jump on the opposition. Have F1 play the reaction of Xd. An aggressive pinch is beaten with a pass off the boards to F3 accelerating towards the NZ. (See Figure 9.5.)

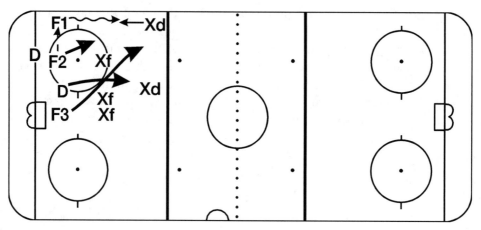

Figure 9.5

A second option against this same face-off alignment is created by a quick give-&-go with the defense. Off the draw, the puck is immediately played back to D1. F2 "allows" the opposing center to chase the puck down low. Quick puck movement up the boards to F1 is supported by the presence of F2. Breaking towards the blue line, Xd will be forced to make a split second decision. Will he surrender the blue line or not? If so, F1 can continue carrying the puck out. If Xd stands up at the blue line, a pass can be headmanned to F2 breaking towards the NZ. (See Figure 9.6.) Note how F3 pulls the middle Xd off the blue line by breaking wide.

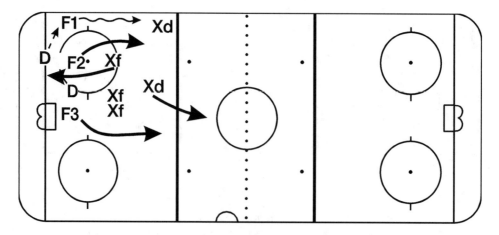

Figure 9.6

Thus far, this chapter has described several different scenarios when a DZ face-off is won. But what of those that are lost? Regardless of the opposition's position-ing, the responsibilities remain constant. When a face-off is lost in the DZ, F2 must tie his man up. Even if the puck is pulled back to Xd on the points, F2 locks on to the opposing center. It is the wings who pressure the points. Either F1 or F3 must get to this area before Xd has time to set up with the puck. Traditionally, both wings will set up off their respective hash marks. Note how D2 positions himself parallel, but to the inside of F3. This allows F3 a clear lane should the puck be drawn back to Xd. In addition, D2 places himself in immediate contact with Xf. (See Figure 9.7.)

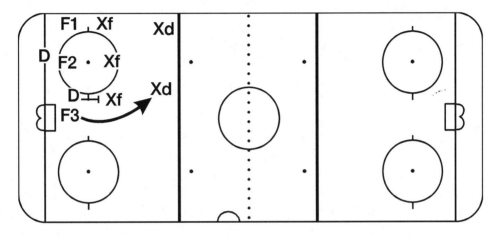

Figure 9.7

Although predominantly used, not all teams adhere to the above model. For example, both the Montreal Canadians and New Jersey Devils position three players along the inside hash mark. F1 and F3 set up immediately next to each other, while D2 lines up just behind F1. Again, both wings have a free lane to Xd, and D2 can easily pick up his assignment. D1 compensates for the freedom given to the opposite side Xf by sliding up near the outside hash mark. He leaves himself a two to three step cushion, should the draw be pulled back. (See Figure 9.8.)

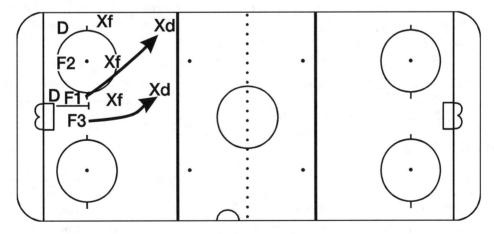

Figure 9.8

Obviously, both D are responsible for Xf driving to the net. Depending on what is designed, the opposition's wings will attempt to get open. Whether the primary play is to crash the net, set up puck-side, or set up off the far post, our D must gain proper position on their assignments and tie their sticks up. (See Figure 9.9.)

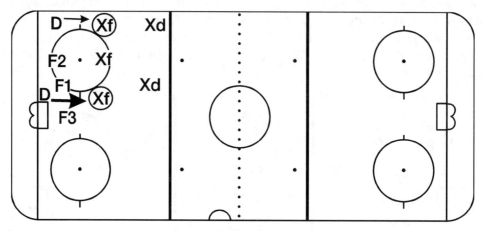

Figure 9.9

Consistent with the chapter on DZ coverage, offensive movements by our own players cannot occur if we do not have puck possession. Do not abandon one's defensive zone responsibilities until it is clear that a teammate will gain control of the puck. Only then can F2 spin off his assignment, while our wings drop below the top of the face-off circles (or take advantage of the opportunity presented by cutting through the NZ) in an attempt to create passing lanes. Because they result in "puck possession," face-offs should be given additional attention when in the DZ for both their defensive and offensive potential.

Neutral Zone Face-Offs

The most interesting aspect of NZ face-offs is that they can occur: a) just "beyond" the DZ; or, b) just "prior to" the OZ. The primary difference in strategy (should the draw be won) is that the first of these requires puck advancement over the red line before firing in deep. Where regrouping and/or headmanning the puck is often obligatory in this situation, it may or not be included in the latter.

In anticipating NZ face-offs, we can expect both teams to line up in standard formation more often than not. (See Figure 9.10.) However, the opposition may slide one Xd parallel to the forwards in extreme circumstances (i.e., late in a period or in need of a goal).

Regrouping

With the draw successfully pulled back, what strategies will enable us to get a jump on the opposition? Much will depend on the time and space created if first moving the puck from D1 to D2. Coaches are asked to review the forward regrouping lanes in Chapter 5 and be creative in modifying for their own team objectives. For example, after sliding F3 to open ice, F1 and F2 can be instructed to interchange at various depths. Be prepared to immediately analyze the opportunities presented before deciding whether to skate or headman the puck. (See Figures 9.11a & 9.11b.)

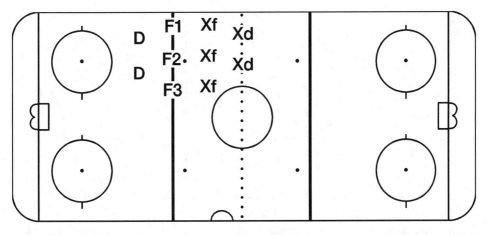

Figure 9.10

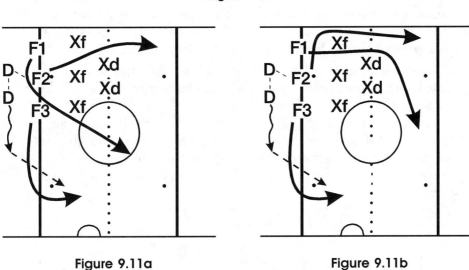

Figure 9.11a   **Figure 9.11b**

Should the opposition be successful in defending against these or any other movements designed to penetrate the OZ with puck control, look to use our wrap or dump plays. (If successful at reaching the puck first, don't forget to use offensive tactics such as second wave attacks with trailers hitting those open seams.)

Direct Headman

Rather than regrouping, suppose we want to force the play more quickly. To accomplish this, many coaches are beginning to reverse the positioning of both the inside wing (here, F3) and same-side defenseman (D2) when lining up for NZ face-offs. The lateral pass, which precedes the longitudinal pass up ice, is rerouted. Instead of passing to his partner, D1 directly headmans to F3 breaking up ice. (See Figure 9.12.)

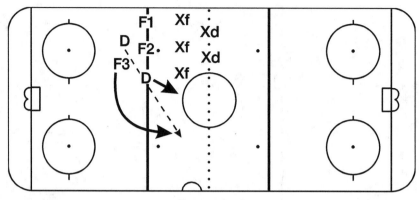

Figure 9.12

This tactic allows for a speedier forward to receive the puck in half the time and effort needed, versus going D to D while the entire unit regroups. Like an RCat, or rapid transition, offense is not initiated after two to three passes, but one headman completion. In addition to the more receptive angle of the pass, F3 is already skating at top speed should he attempt to dump or penetrate into the OZ.

If the draw is lost, a quick interchange back to the original positions can be accomplished without forfeiting much. The immediate proximity allows D2 to lock on to his assignment, while his partner retrieves the puck. Often this inside wing will exist as the primary outlet and attempt to break wide. Proper positioning and anticipation by D2 negates this wide option. Using a standard alignment, F2 attempts to take away the regroup option by positioning himself between both opposing defensemen. In this situation, however, F3 has a clear lane to pressure Xd. (See Figure 9.13.)

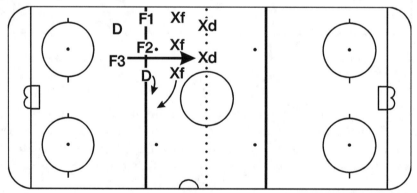

Figure 9.13

Offensive Zone Face-Offs

Two questions immediately come to mind when diagramming OZ face-offs. First, where do we want to go with the puck? Do we want to push it to the net or pull it back to the points? As a result, how should we line up, and what are the subsequent roles of each player? Remember, the positioning of our players is not limited to the hash marks, but anywhere behind the hash marks.

A. A standard formation means that at puck level, the opposition will possess a man-advantage. They will line up four players (3 forwards and 1 defenseman) against our three forwards.

In most cases, the primary offensive play will be to pull the puck back to our points who will maneuvre to create either a passing or shooting lane. Because of this, it is not uncommon to slide D1 to the top of the face-off circle. Rather than waiting, he may be able to get a quicker jump on the puck. In addition, both our wings may be instructed to back off the hash marks in an attempt to create skating and/or stickhandling room. (See Figure 9.14.) F3 can even be instructed to set up in the high slot and drive to the net at full speed as the puck is dropped. Though difficult to defend against, the timing of such aggressive movements needs to be practiced.

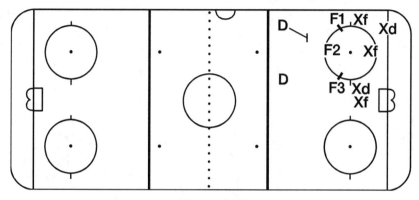

Figure 9.14

The key to success will be twofold. Obviously, we must win the draw. For this reason, it is not uncommon to put two centers out on the ice late in a period/game. This allows the first to play very aggressively. If he is kicked out, or is able to get the opposing centerman kicked out, we still have another center to take the draw. If not won cleanly, F1 has been taught (in all three zones) to tap the puck back to the points while F2 ties up the opposing center. The head start created by playing off the hash mark makes this play much easier. Note how it is always the outside wing who assumes this duty. After playing the puck back in the DZ and NZ, F1 is able to continue his line to open ice. Here in the OZ, his movement behind F2 helps to place him in front of the opposition's net. Furthermore, this anticipated movement allows the inside wing (F3) to fulfill his role comprising the second key to success. Namely, to screen the opposing wing's access to our points before driving to the net. Although lining up directly across from Xd, a quick lateral step can impede the forward progress of Xf and force him to take a wider lane to the outside. (See Figure 9.15.)

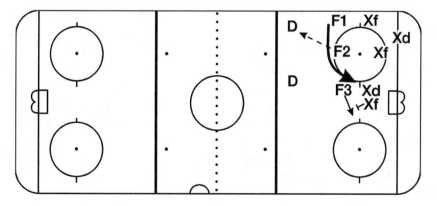

Figure 9.15

Let us assume that F2 has successfully pulled the draw back to D1. F3 need not worry about Xd, for most teams will not send a defenseman to pressure the points. As mentioned, focus is placed on momentarily screening out the adjacent wing. Whether or not our own D will play their "off" side on OZ face-offs is up to the coaching staff. If you possess a defenseman who is particularly accurate when firing one-timers, you may look to exploit this talent. Should D1 not have a clear shooting lane, passing to his partner shifts the play to the middle lanes while both F1 and F3 drive to the net. Allow F2 to position himself according to coverage provided by the opposing center. If left alone, F2 may be able to slide back and set up off the original face-off circle. Otherwise, he too can take a lane to the net by skating behind and positioning himself off the puck-side post. (See Figure 9.16.)

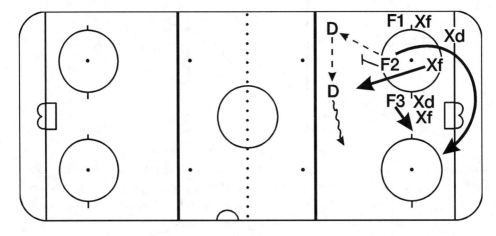

Figure 9.16

B. Rather than D1, we can shift F1 from his board-side position to the top of the face-off circle. This allows D2 to crash the slot area, while not sacrificing a presence at the blue line. In addition to immediately putting the puck on net, F2 has the option of passing laterally to an accelerating D2. As a result, D1 slides over to cover the vacant middle lane while F2 slides back to cover the point area. In most cases, D2 will be advised to stop in the high slot rather than following his shot in deep. The roles of both F2 and F3 remain as before. Give teammates time to set up by momentarily screening out assignments, before driving to the net. (See Figure 9.17.)

Note: This alignment is also conducive to quickly setting up our forecheck, should the draw be lost. F2 flushes behind the net. The inside wing (F3), takes away any wide outlet by getting to the opposite side boards. Due to his positioning, the board-side/high wing (F1) can quickly assume middle lane coverage.

C. Similar to a powerplay sharing the same objective, a face-off alignment can attempt to overload a specific area of ice. Here, both wings line up along the inside hash mark. With Xf instructed to pressure the points, we create a man-advantage situation in the slot. The entire unit must recognize the options created by the "shot" of F2. If on his forehand, F2 can attempt to push the puck towards the area flooded by our wings. Here, both F1 and F3 drive to the net, versus only one Xd. (See Figure 9.18a.) If on his backhand, he can pull the puck back to D2. This

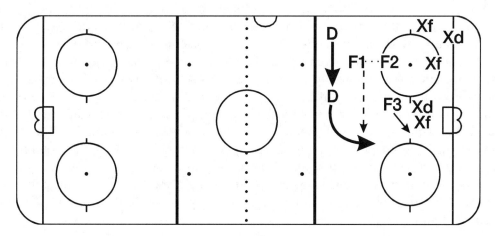

Figure 9.17

motion may be made easier by reversing the bottom-hand grip on the hockey stick. Should F2 be a right-hand shot taking an OZ face-off on the left side, holding the stick with both palms facing down may increase the leverage needed to pull the puck back. Note how this formation allows F1 and F3 to screen the opposition's access to the blue line while creating open lanes. (See Figure 9.18b.)

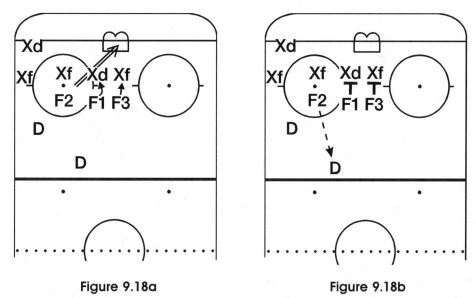

Figure 9.18a   **Figure 9.18b**

In both scenarios, we must nullify the presence of Xf positioned along the boards. This is most successfully accomplished by positioning D1 at the top of the face-off circle. Here, Xf can be screened out while D1 simultaneously maintains a defensive posture should the draw be lost. Because Xf may have some room, it makes little sense to play the puck to that side of the ice. Our goal is to direct puck movement to that area already occupied by our forwards. Again, F2 positions himself in accordance with the coverage of the opposing center. Remember, scoring opportunities and continued puck control following OZ face-offs depend on the ability of the entire unit to create time and space.

It is emphatically reminded that face-offs are by no means limited to the forma-tions detailed in this chapter — no matter in which zone they occur. Coaches can line units up anywhere on their own side of the hash marks and are encouraged to modify according to team strengths and weaknesses. The strategies provided sim-ply represent those frequently used at the prep school level and beyond. Move-ments and tactics such as playing the puck forward or backward, and defensemen lining up on their "off-side," remain the decision of the coaching staff. It is hoped that consideration and implementation of the discussed principles will assist in developing a foundation for your team's system. Do not overlook the potential of face-offs. In an attempt to keep their importance in perspective, I often remind my players that the effort required to penetrate, work along the boards, dig the puck out, and create scoring opportunities, all may be accomplished within the split second required to win a face-off.

Face-Offs: A Summary

Player movement following all face-offs is dependent on three factors:

1. The alignment of our unit...versus the opposition.

2. Whether the preconceived play is to push the puck forward or pull it back.

3. Whether the draw is won or lost.

In the DZ:

if won ...

a. Versus a standard (3-2) formation, reverse the play and utilize the far open lane. Quick puck movement behind the net is complemented with a headman outlet skating to the opposite side boards.

b. Versus an overload formation, utilize the open board-side wing. If Xd pinches, play the puck up to the NZ in anticipation of accelerating teammates.

if lost ...

a. F2 must lock on the opposing center.

b. F1 and F3 are responsible for pressuring the points.

c. D1 and D2 are responsible for boxing out the opposing wings.

In the NZ:

if won...

a. If on our side of the red line, look to regroup.

b. If on their side of the red line, get the puck deep. (Wrap/Dump to opposite corner.)

if lost...

a. F2 attempt to gain position between both Xd (to prevent regroup option).

b. F1 and F3 hold up opposing wings.

c. D1 retrieve puck, while partner looks to hold up opposing center.

In the OZ:

if won ...

a. Using a standard formation, feed points while forwards establish position around net.

b. Using an overload, look to shoot or feed weak-side D crashing slot area.

if lost ...

a. F2 pressure Xd to move puck quickly.

b. Middle lane wing get to outlet area along far-side boards.

c. Board-side/High wing get to outlet area in middle lane.

d. Both D can look to pinch ... if supported.

Teaching Special Teams Play

A progressive approach to teaching special teams play is necessary due to the coordinated movements of all involved. Tactics such as rotating, interchanging, cycling, etc., all involve primary movements supported by secondary movements. The disciplined elements of passing, positioning, penetration, and patience offer the foundation for success — when executed together. It is our goal as coaches, to achieve this level of play.

Follow these guidelines when introducing this facet of play:

Step 1. Familiarity breeds Confidence.

Design team drills without opposition. Emphasis should be placed on both puck and player movement.

Step 2. Read, React, and Create Situations.

Design team drills in specific zones, while gradually increasing opposition. Players will begin to recognize certain patterns of play assumed by various positions. The advantage gained by knowing how most defensemen and/or forwards play these situations can be a great cognitive addition to any team.

Step 3. Movement with a Purpose.

Allow for puck movement over the entire ice surface to include all elements of play. Transitions from defense to offense, and vice versa, should be emphasized. Because of the man-advantage (or disadvantage) situation, players may begin to test different scenario outcomes. Allow for this exploration, but use it as a learning experience. Mistakes made should be immediately pointed out and corrected.

Step 4. Poise under Pressure.

Special teams play involves pressure. Whether on the powerplay, killing a penalty, or lining up for a face-off, a mistake can prove quite costly. Continued practice combined with productive feedback can help transfer one's confidence to game situations. Under this stage, drills are paced at a much greater speed, and there is more pressure to move the puck.

Step 5. Game Conditions.

Plan a controlled scrimmage aimed at special teams play. Have players be prepared to stop on the whistle in order to correct positional problems and demonstrate alternate movements designed to achieve the primary objective.

Notes

Notes